THE
American Patriot's
HANDBOOK

D1622727

Printed Especially for

"The Family Fraternity"®

WOODMEN OF THE WORLD/OMAHA WOODMEN
LIFE INSURANCE SOCIETY

Omaha, Nebraska

Contents

⊕ RAND McNALLY
Copyright ©1997 Rand McNally
Printed in U.S.A.

PART I

THE

Constitution

OF OUR UNITED STATES

The Constitution of our United States
The Declaration of Independence
Lincoln's Gettysburg Address

CONTENTS

Note: For the convenience of the reader, headings, subheadings in italics, notes and cross references have been inserted in the Constitution and the Declaration of Independence, and the signers of the latter document have been classified by states. The capitalization, punctuation, and spelling have been modernized, but care has been taken to make no changes which would alter the meaning of the original texts.

These two famous documents may be seen in facsimile on pages 11 and 59.

3

A reproduction of Rossiter's painting of the Constitutional Convention,

actually portraying its members. The original hangs in Independence Hall.

GEORGE
WASHINGTON

BENJAMIN
FRANKLIN

ALEXANDER
HAMILTON

JAMES MADISON

Washington presided over the Constitutional Convention; Franklin was the oldest and most experienced statesman in the assembly; Hamilton's brilliant young mind was a challenge to his colleagues; Madison has often been called the "Father of the Constitution," and he also led in securing the adoption of its first ten amendments.

THE CONSTITUTION
OF THE
UNITED STATES OF AMERICA

PREAMBLE

WE THE PEOPLE of the United States in order to form a more perfect union, establish justice, insure domestic tranquillity, provide for the common defense, promote the general welfare, and secure the blessings of liberty to ourselves and our posterity, do ordain and establish this Constitution for the United States of America.

THE LEGISLATIVE DEPARTMENT

ARTICLE I

SECTION 1. All legislative powers herein granted shall be vested in a Congress of the United States, which shall consist of a Senate and House of Representatives.

How the House of Representatives Is Formed

SECTION 2. The House of Representatives shall be composed of members chosen every second year by the people of the several States, and the electors in each State shall have the qualifications requisite for electors of the most numerous branch of the State Legislature.

No person shall be a Representative who shall not have attained to the age of twenty-five years, and been seven years a citizen of the United States, and who shall not, when elected, be an inhabitant of that State in which he shall be chosen.

Representatives and direct taxes shall be apportioned among the several States which may be included within this Union, according to their respective numbers, which shall be determined by adding to the whole number of free persons, including those bound to service for a term of years, and excluding Indians not taxed, three-fifths of all other persons. The actual enumeration shall be made within three years after the first meeting of the Congress of the United States, and within every subsequent term of ten years, in such manner as they shall by law direct. The number of Representatives shall not exceed one for every thirty thousand, but each State shall have at least one Representative; and until such enumeration shall be made, the State of New Hampshire shall be entitled to choose three, Massachusetts eight, Rhode Island and Providence Plantations one, Connecticut five, New York six, New Jersey four, Pennsylvania eight, Delaware one, Maryland six, Virginia ten, North Carolina five, South Carolina five, and Georgia three.

(See also Amendment XIV, Section 2, page 35.)

When vacancies happen in the representation from any State, the executive authority thereof shall issue writs of election to fill such vacancies.

The House of Representatives shall choose their Speaker and other officers; and shall have the sole power of impeachment.

How the Senate Is Formed

SECTION 3. The Senate of the United States shall be composed of two Senators from each State, chosen by the Legislature thereof, for six years; and each Senator shall have one vote.

Immediately after they shall be assembled in consequence of the first election, they shall be divided as equally as may be into three classes. The seats of the Senators of the first class shall be vacated at the expiration of the second year, of the second class at the expiration of the fourth year, and of the third class at the expiration of the sixth year, so that one-third may be chosen every second year; and if vacancies happen by resignation, or otherwise, during the recess of the Legislature of any State, the Executive thereof may make temporary appointments until the next meeting of the Legislature, which shall then fill such vacancies.

(*See also Amendment XVII, page 37.*)

No person shall be a Senator who shall not have attained to the age of thirty years, and been nine years a citizen of the United States, and who shall not, when elected, be an inhabitant of that State for which he shall be chosen.

The Vice President of the United States shall be President of the Senate, but shall have no vote unless they be equally divided.

The Senate shall choose their other officers, and also a president *pro tempore*, in the absence of the Vice President, or when he shall exercise the office of President of the United States.

The Senate shall have the sole power to try all impeachments. When sitting for that purpose, they shall be on oath or affirmation. When the President of the United States is tried, the Chief Justice shall preside, and no person shall be convicted without the concurrence of two-thirds of the members present.

Judgment in cases of impeachment shall not extend further than to removal from office, and disqualification to hold and enjoy any office of honor, trust, or profit under the United States; but the party convicted shall nevertheless be liable and subject to indictment, trial, judgment, and punishment, according to law.

Congressional Elections: Time of Assembling

SECTION 4. The times, places, and manner of holding elections for Senators and Representatives shall be prescribed in each State by the Legislature thereof; but the Congress may at any time by law make or alter such regulations, except as to the places of choosing Senators.

The Congress shall assemble at least once in every year, and such meeting shall be on the first Monday in December, unless they shall by law appoint a different day.

(See also Amendment XX, Section 2, page 39.)

Rules and Procedure of Congress

SECTION 5. Each House shall be the judge of the elections, returns, and qualifications of its own members, and a majority of each shall constitute a quorum to do business; but a smaller number may adjourn from day to day, and may be authorized to compel the attendance of absent members, in such manner and under such penalties as each House may provide.

Each House may determine the rules of its proceedings, punish its members for disorderly behavior, and, with the concurrence of two-thirds, expel a member.

Each House shall keep a journal of its proceedings, and from time to time publish the same, excepting such parts as

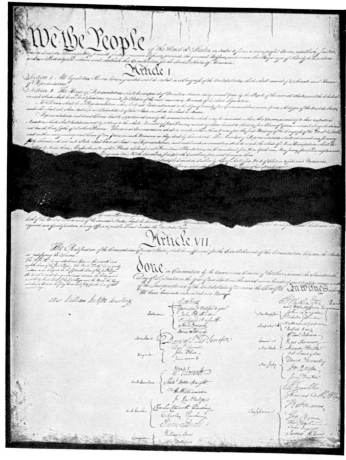

This facsimile of the first and last portions of the original draft of the Constitution shows (above) the preamble and part of Article I, and (below) Article VII and signatures. The original, under constant guard, is in the Library of Congress.

may in their judgment require secrecy; and the yeas and nays of the members of either House on any question shall, at the desire of one-fifth of those present, be entered on the journal.

Neither House, during the session of Congress, shall, without the consent of the other, adjourn for more than three days, nor to any other place than that in which the two Houses shall be sitting.

Privileges and Restrictions of Congressmen

SECTION 6.   The Senators and Representatives shall receive a compensation for their services, to be ascertained by law and paid out of the Treasury of the United States.   They shall in all cases, except treason, felony, and breach of the peace, be privileged from arrest during their attendance at the session of their respective Houses, and in going to and returning from the same; and for any speech or debate in either House they shall not be questioned in any other place.

No Senator or Representative shall, during the time for which he was elected, be appointed to any civil office under the authority of the United States, which shall have been created, or the emoluments whereof shall have been increased during such time; and no person holding any office under the United States shall be a member of either House during his continuance in office.

How Federal Laws Are Made

SECTION 7.   All bills for raising revenue shall originate in the House of Representatives; but the Senate may propose or concur with amendments as on other bills.

Every bill which shall have passed the House of Representatives and the Senate shall, before it become a law, be presented to the President of the United States; if he approve he shall sign it, but if not he shall return it with his objections to that House in which it shall have originated, who shall enter the objections at large on their journal and proceed to reconsider it. If after such reconsideration two-thirds of that House shall agree to pass the bill, it shall be sent, together with the objections, to the other House, by which it shall likewise be reconsidered, and if approved by two-thirds of that House, it shall become a law. But in all such cases the votes of both Houses shall be determined by yeas and nays, and the names of the persons voting for and against the bill shall be entered on the journal of each House respectively. If any bill shall not be returned by the President within ten days (Sundays excepted) after it shall have been presented to him, the same shall be a law, in like manner as if he had signed it, unless the Congress by their adjournment prevent its return, in which case it shall not be a law.

Every order, resolution, or vote to which the concurrence of the Senate and House of Representatives may be necessary (except on a question of adjournment) shall be presented to the President of the United States; and before the same shall take effect, shall be approved by him, or being disapproved by him shall be repassed by two-thirds of the Senate and House of Representatives, according to the rules and limitations prescribed in the case of a bill.

Powers Granted to Congress

Section 8. The Congress shall have power to lay and collect taxes, duties, imposts and excises, to pay the debts and provide for the common defense and general welfare of the United States; but all duties, imposts and excises shall be uniform throughout the United States;

To borrow money on the credit of the United States;

To regulate commerce with foreign nations, and among the several States, and with the Indian tribes;

To establish an uniform rule of naturalization, and uniform laws on the subject of bankruptcies throughout the United States;

To coin money, regulate the value thereof and of foreign coin, and fix the standard of weights and measures;

To provide for the punishment of counterfeiting the securities and current coin of the United States;

To establish post offices and post roads;

To promote the progress of science and useful arts, by securing for limited times to authors and inventors the exclusive right to their respective writings and discoveries;

To constitute tribunals inferior to the Supreme Court;

To define and punish piracies and felonies committed on the high seas, and offenses against the law of nations;

To declare war, grant letters of marque and reprisal, and make rules concerning captures on land and water;

To raise and support armies, but no appropriation of money to that use shall be for a longer term than two years;

To provide and maintain a navy;

To make rules for the government and regulation of the land and naval forces;

To provide for calling forth the militia to execute the laws of the Union, suppress insurrections and repel invasions;

To provide for organizing, arming, and disciplining the militia, and for governing such part of them as may be employed in the service of the United States, reserving to the States respectively, the appointment of the officers, and the authority of training the militia according to the discipline prescribed by Congress;

To exercise exclusive legislation, in all cases whatsoever,

over such district (not exceeding ten miles square) as may, by cession of particular States, and the acceptance of Congress, become the seat of the government of the United States; and to exercise like authority over all places purchased by the consent of the Legislature of the State in which the same shall be, for the erection of forts, magazines, arsenals, dockyards, and other needful buildings;—and

To make all laws which shall be necessary and proper for carrying into execution the foregoing powers, and all other powers vested by this Constitution in the government of the United States, or in any department or officer thereof.

Powers Denied to Federal Government

SECTION 9. The migration or importation of such persons as any of the States now existing shall think proper to admit, shall not be prohibited by the Congress prior to the year one thousand eight hundred and eight, but a tax or duty may be imposed on such importation, not exceeding ten dollars for each person.

The privilege of the writ of *habeas corpus* shall not be suspended, unless when in cases of rebellion or invasion the public safety may require it.

No bill of attainder or *ex post facto* law shall be passed.

No capitation or other direct tax shall be laid, unless in proportion to the census or enumeration hereinbefore directed to be taken.

No tax or duty shall be laid on articles exported from any State.

No preference shall be given by any regulation of commerce or revenue to the ports of one State over those of another; nor shall vessels, bound to or from one State, be obliged to enter, clear, or pay duties in another.

No money shall be drawn from the Treasury, but in consequence of appropriations made by law; and a regular statement and account of the receipts and expenditures of all public money shall be published from time to time.

No title of nobility shall be granted by the United States; and no person holding any office of profit or trust under them shall, without the consent of the Congress, accept of any present, emolument, office, or title, of any kind whatever, from any king, prince, or foreign state.

Powers Denied to State Governments

SECTION 10.   No State shall enter into any treaty, alliance, or confederation; grant letters of marque and reprisal; coin money; emit bills of credit; make anything but gold and silver coin a tender in payment of debts; pass any bill of attainder, *ex post facto* law, or law impairing the obligation of contracts, or grant any title of nobility.

No State shall, without the consent of the Congress, lay any imposts or duties on imports or exports, except what may be absolutely necessary for executing its inspection laws; and the net produce of all duties and imposts, laid by any State on imports or exports, shall be for the use of the Treasury of the United States; and all such laws shall be subject to the revision and control of the Congress.

No State shall, without the consent of Congress, lay any duty of tonnage, keep troops, or ships of war in time of peace, enter into any agreement or compact with another State, or with a foreign power, or engage in war, unless actually invaded or in such imminent danger as will not admit of delay.

THE EXECUTIVE DEPARTMENT

Article II

The President and Vice President

Section 1. The executive power shall be vested in a President of the United States of America. He shall hold his office during the term of four years, and together with the Vice President, chosen for the same term, be elected as follows:

The Electoral College

Each State shall appoint, in such manner as the Legislature thereof may direct, a number of Electors equal to the whole number of Senators and Representatives to which the State may be entitled in the Congress; but no Senator or Representative, or person holding an office of trust or profit under the United States, shall be appointed an Elector.

The Electors shall meet in their respective States, and vote by ballot for two persons, of whom one at least shall not be an inhabitant of the same State with themselves. And they shall make a list of all the persons voted for, and of the number of votes for each; which list they shall sign and certify, and transmit sealed to the seat of the government of the United States, directed to the President of the Senate. The President of the Senate shall, in the presence of the Senate and House of Representatives, open all the certificates, and the votes shall then be counted. The person having the greatest number of votes shall be the President, if such number be a majority of the whole number of Electors appointed; and if there be more than one who have such majority, and have an equal number of votes, then the

In this house on Cherry Street, in New York City, Washington lived from April, 1789, to February, 1790.

The White House, Washington, D. C., which, with its predecessor (burned by the British in 1814), has been the residence of the Presidents of the United States since November 8, 1800.

House of Representatives shall immediately choose by ballot one of them for President; and if no person have a majority, then from the five highest on the list the said House shall in like manner choose the President. But in choosing the President, the votes shall be taken by States, the representation from each State having one vote; a quorum for this purpose shall consist of a member or members from two-thirds of the States, and a majority of all the States shall be necessary to a choice. In every case, after the choice of the President, the person having the greatest number of votes of the Electors shall be the Vice President. But if there should remain two or more who have equal votes, the Senate shall choose from them by ballot the Vice President. *(See also Amendments XII and XX, pages 32 and 39.)*

The Congress may determine the time of choosing the Electors, and the day on which they shall give their votes; which day shall be the same throughout the United States.

Qualifications, Succession by Vice President, Salary, and Oath of the President

No person except a natural-born citizen, or a citizen of the United States at the time of the adoption of this Constitution, shall be eligible to the office of President; neither shall any person be eligible to that office who shall not have attained to the age of thirty-five years, and been fourteen years a resident within the United States.

In case of the removal of the President from office, or of his death, resignation, or inability to discharge the powers and duties of the said office, the same shall devolve on the Vice President, and the Congress may by law provide for the case of removal, death, resignation, or inability, both of the President and Vice President, declaring what officer shall then act as President, and such officer shall act accordingly, until the disability be removed or a President shall be elected.

The President shall, at stated times, receive for his services a compensation, which shall neither be increased nor diminished during the period for which he shall have been elected, and he shall not receive within that period any other emolument from the United States, or any of them.

Before he enter on the execution of his office, he shall take the following oath or affirmation: "I do solemnly swear (or affirm) that I will faithfully execute the office of President of the United States, and will, to the best of my ability, preserve, protect, and defend the Constitution of the United States."

Military and Pardoning Powers of the President

SECTION 2. The President shall be commander in chief of the army and navy of the United States, and of the militia of the several States when called into the actual service of the United States; he may require the opinion, in writing, of the principal officer in each of the executive departments, upon any subject relating to the duties of their respective offices, and he shall have power to grant reprieves and pardons for offenses against the United States, except in cases of impeachment.

Treaties and Appointments by President and Senate

He shall have power, by and with the advice and consent of the Senate, to make treaties, provided two-thirds of the Senators present concur; and he shall nominate, and, by and with the advice and consent of the Senate, shall appoint ambassadors, other public ministers and consuls, judges of the Supreme Court, and all other officers of the United States whose appointments are not herein otherwise provided for, and which shall be established by law; but the Congress may by law vest the appointment of such inferior officers, as they think proper, in the President alone, in the courts of law, or in the heads of departments.

The President shall have power to fill up all vacancies that may happen during the recess of the Senate, by granting commissions which shall expire at the end of their next session.

The Executive and Other Duties of the President

SECTION 3. He shall from time to time give to the Congress information of the state of the Union, and recommend to their consideration such measures as he shall judge necessary and expedient; he may, on extraordinary occasions, convene both Houses, or either of them, and in case of disagreement between them, with respect to the time of adjournment, he may adjourn them to such time as he shall think proper; he shall receive ambassadors and other public ministers; he shall take care that the laws be faithfully executed, and shall commission all the officers of the United States.

Removal of Executive Officers from Office

SECTION 4. The President, Vice President, and all civil officers of the United States shall be removed from office on impeachment for, and conviction of, treason, bribery, or other high crimes and misdemeanors.

THE JUDICIAL DEPARTMENT

ARTICLE III

The Federal Courts; the Tenure and Salary of Judges

SECTION 1. The judicial power of the United States shall be vested in one Supreme Court, and in such inferior courts as the Congress may from time to time ordain and establish. The judges, both of the Supreme and inferior courts, shall hold their offices during good behavior, and shall, at stated times, receive for their services a compensation, which shall not be diminished during their continuance in office.

Jurisdiction of Federal Courts in General

SECTION 2. The judicial power shall extend to all cases in law and equity arising under this Constitution, the laws of the United States, and treaties made, or which shall be made, under their authority; to all cases affecting ambassadors, other public ministers and consuls; to all cases of admiralty and maritime jurisdiction; to controversies to which the United States shall be a party; to controversies between two or more States; between a State and citizens of another State; between citizens of different States; between citizens of the same State claiming lands under grants of different States, and between a State, or the citizens thereof, and foreign states, citizens or subjects. (*See also Amendment XI, page 32.*)

Jurisdiction of Supreme Court

In all cases affecting ambassadors, other public ministers and consuls, and those in which a State shall be party, the Supreme Court shall have original jurisdiction. **In all** the other cases before mentioned, the Supreme Court **shall** have appellate jurisdiction, both as to law and fact, with such exceptions and under such regulations as the Congress shall make.

Trial by Jury

The trial of all crimes, except in cases of impeachment, shall be by jury; and such trial shall be held in the State where the said crimes shall have been committed; but when not committed within any State, the trial shall be at such place or places as the Congress may by law have directed.

Treason: Its Definition and Punishment

SECTION 3. Treason against the United States shall consist only in levying war against them, or in adhering to their enemies, giving them aid and comfort. No person shall be convicted of treason unless on the testimony of two witnesses to the same overt act, or on confession in open court.

The Congress shall have power to declare the punishment of treason, but no attainder of treason shall work corruption of blood, or forfeiture except during the life of the person attainted.

RELATIONSHIP BETWEEN FEDERAL AND STATE GOVERNMENTS

ARTICLE IV

Faith and Credit between States

SECTION 1. Full faith and credit shall be given in each State to the public acts, records, and judicial proceedings of every other State. And the Congress may by general laws prescribe the manner in which such acts, records, and proceedings shall be proved, and the effect thereof.

Interstate Comity regarding Citizens and Other Persons

SECTION 2. The citizens of each State shall be entitled to all privileges and immunities of citizens in the several States.

A person charged in any State with treason, felony, or other crime, who shall flee from justice and be found in another State, shall, on demand of the executive authority of the State from which he fled, be delivered up, to be removed to the State having jurisdiction of the crime.

No person held to service or labor in one State, under the laws thereof, escaping into another, shall, in consequence of any law or regulation therein, be discharged from such service or labor, but shall be delivered up on claim of the party to whom such service or labor may be due.

Admission of New States to the Union

SECTION 3. New States may be admitted by the Congress into this Union; but no new State shall be formed or erected within the jurisdiction of any other State; nor any State be formed by the junction of two or more States, or parts of States, without the consent of the Legislatures of the States concerned as well as of the Congress.

Congress Makes Rules respecting Government Property

The Congress shall have power to dispose of and make all needful rules and regulations respecting the territory or other property belonging to the United States; and nothing in this Constitution shall be so construed as to prejudice any claims of the United States or of any particular State.

SECTION 4. The United States shall guarantee to every State in this Union a republican form of government, and shall protect each of them against invasion; and on application of the Legislature, or of the Executive (when the Legislature cannot be convened), against domestic violence.

PROVISIONS FOR AMENDMENTS
ARTICLE V

The Congress, whenever two-thirds of both Houses shall deem it necessary, shall propose amendments to this Constitution, or, on the application of the Legislatures of two-thirds of the several States, shall call a convention for proposing amendments, which, in either case, shall be valid to all intents and purposes, as part of this Constitution, when ratified by the Legislatures of three-fourths of the several States, or by conventions in three-fourths thereof, as the one or the other mode of ratification may be proposed by the Congress; provided that no amendment which may be made prior to the year one thousand eight hundred and eight shall in any manner affect the first and fourth clauses in the ninth section of the first article; and that no State, without its consent, shall be deprived of its equal suffrage in the Senate.

THE CONSTITUTION, THE SUPREME LAW OF THE LAND
ARTICLE VI
Prior Debts

All debts contracted and engagements entered into, before the adoption of this Constitution, shall be as valid against the United States under this Constitution as under the Confederation.

The Supreme Law of the Land and the Obligation of State Judges

This Constitution, and the laws of the United States which shall be made in pursuance thereof; and all treaties made, or which shall be made, under the authority of the United States, shall be the supreme law of the land; and the judges in every State shall be bound thereby, anything in the Constitution or laws of any State to the contrary notwithstanding.

Federal and State Officers Bound by Oath to Support the Constitution

The Senators and Representatives before mentioned, and the members of the several State Legislatures, and all executive and judicial officers, both of the United States and of the several States, shall be bound by oath or affirmation to support this Constitution; but no religious test shall ever be required as a qualification to any office or public trust under the United States.

PROVISIONS FOR RATIFICATION BY STATES

ARTICLE VII

The ratification of the conventions of nine states shall be sufficient for the establishment of this Constitution between the States so ratifying the same.

Done in convention by the unanimous consent of the States present, the seventeenth day of September in the year of our Lord one thousand seven hundred and eighty seven, and of

*the independence of the United States of America the twelfth.
In witness whereof we have hereunto subscribed our names.*

Attest: WILLAM JACKSON,
         Secretary

Go: WASHINGTON — *Presidt.*
    and Deputy from Virginia

Delaware
GEO: READ
GUNNING BEDFORD, JUN
JOHN DICKINSON
RICHARD BASSETT
JACO: BROOM

New Hampshire
JOHN LANGDON
NICHOLAS GILMAN

Massachusetts
NATHANIEL GORHAM
RUFUS KING

Maryland
JAMES MCHENRY
DAN OF ST. THOS. JENIFER
DANL. CARROLL

Connecticut
WM. SAML. JOHNSON
ROGER SHERMAN

Virginia
JOHN BLAIR—
JAMES MADISON, JR.

New York
ALEXANDER HAMILTON

North Carolina
WM. BLOUNT
RICHD. DOBBS SPAIGHT
HU WILLIAMSON

New Jersey
WIL: LIVINGSTON
DAVID BREARLEY
WM. PATERSON
JONA: DAYTON

South Carolina
J. RUTLEDGE
CHARLES COTESWORTH
  PINCKNEY
CHARLES PINCKNEY
PIERCE BUTLER

Pennsylvania
B. FRANKLIN
THOMAS MIFFLIN
ROBT. MORRIS
GEO. CLYMER
THOS. FITZSIMONS
JARED INGERSOLL
JAMES WILSON
GOUV MORRIS

Georgia
WILLIAM FEW
ABR BALDWIN

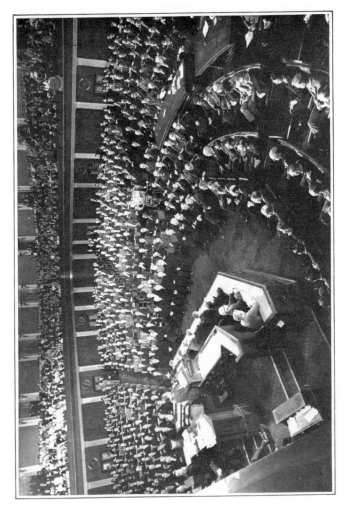

The President, delivering his message to the ninety-third Congress, in joint session

THE AMENDMENTS
TO THE CONSTITUTION

The first ten amendments to the Constitution, known as "A Bill of Rights," were adopted by the first Congress, called to meet in New York City, March 4, 1789. They were later ratified by the various States, and on December 15, 1791, were made a part of the Constitution.

AMENDMENT I

Freedom of Religion, Speech, and the Press; Right of Assembly and Petition

CONGRESS shall make no law respecting an establishment of religion, or prohibiting the free exercise thereof; or abridging the freedom of speech, or of the press, or the right of the people peaceably to assemble, and to petition the government for a redress of grievances.

AMENDMENT II

Right to Keep and Bear Arms

A well regulated militia, being necessary to the security of a free state, the right of the people to keep and bear arms shall not be infringed.

AMENDMENT III

Quartering of Soldiers

No soldier shall in time of peace be quartered in any

house without the consent of the owner, nor in time of war, but in a manner to be prescribed by law.

AMENDMENT IV

Regulation of Right of Search and Seizure

The right of the people to be secure in their persons, houses, papers, and effects, against unreasonable searches and seizures, shall not be violated, and no warrants shall issue but upon probable cause, supported by oath or affirmation, and particularly describing the place to be searched and the persons or things to be seized.

AMENDMENT V

Protection for Persons and Their Property

No person shall be held to answer for a capital or other-wise infamous crime, unless on a presentment or indictment of a grand jury, except in cases arising in the land or naval forces, or in the militia, when in actual service in time of war or public danger; nor shall any person be subject for the same offense to be twice put in jeopardy of life or limb; nor shall be compelled in any criminal case to be a witness against himself, nor be deprived of life, liberty, or property, without due process of law; nor shall private property be taken for public use, without just compensation.

AMENDMENT VI

Rights of Persons Accused of Crime

In all criminal prosecutions, the accused shall enjoy the right to a speedy and public trial by an impartial jury of the State and district wherein the crime shall have been committed, which district shall have been previously ascertained by law, and to be informed of the nature and cause of the accusation; to be confronted with the witnesses against him; to have compulsory process for obtaining witnesses in his favor, and to have the assistance of counsel for his defense.

AMENDMENT VII

Right of Trial by Jury in Suits at Common Law

In suits at common law, where the value in controversy shall exceed twenty dollars, the right of trial by jury shall be preserved, and no fact tried by a jury shall be otherwise re-examined in any court of the United States, than according to the rules of the common law.

AMENDMENT VIII

Protection Against Excessive Bail and Punishments

Excessive bail shall not be required, nor excessive fines imposed, nor cruel and unusual punishments inflicted.

AMENDMENT IX

Constitution Does Not List All Individual Rights

The enumeration in the Constitution of certain rights shall not be construed to deny or disparage others retained by the people.

AMENDMENT X

Powers Reserved to the States and the People

The powers not delegated to the United States by the Constitution, nor prohibited by it to the States, are reserved to the States respectively, or to the people.

Amendment XI

Limitation of Power of Federal Courts

The eleventh amendment, adopted by the third Congress, held in Philadelphia, 1794, was ratified by three-fourths of the States, and made a part of the Constitution, January 8, 1798.

The judicial power of the United States shall not be construed to extend to any suit in law or equity, commenced or prosecuted against one of the United States by citizens of another State, or by citizens or subjects of any foreign state. *(See Article III, Section 2, page 22.)*

Amendment XII

Regulation of Electoral College

The twelfth amendment, adopted by the eighth Congress, held in Washington, D. C., 1803, was ratified by three-fourths of the States, and made a part of the Constitution, September 25, 1804. This amendment was proposed to replace paragraph 3, Section 1, Article II, of the original Constitution. (See pages 17, 39 and 40.)

The Electors shall meet in their respective States and vote by ballot for President and Vice President, one of whom, at least, shall not be an inhabitant of the same State with themselves; they shall name in their ballots the person voted for as President, and in distinct ballots the person voted for as Vice President, and they shall make distinct lists of all persons voted for as President, and of all persons voted for as Vice President, and of the number of votes for each, which lists they shall sign and certify, and transmit sealed to the seat of the government of the United States, directed to the President of the Senate. The President of the Senate shall, in the presence of the Senate and House of Representatives, open all the certificates, and the votes shall then be counted. The person having the greatest number of votes for President shall be the President, if such number be a majority of the whole number of Electors appointed; and if no person have such majority, then from the persons having the highest numbers not exceeding three on the list of those voted for as President, the House of Representatives shall choose immediately, by ballot, the President. But in choosing the President the votes shall be taken by States, the representation from each State having one vote; a quorum for this purpose shall consist of a member or members from two-thirds of the States, and a majority of all the States shall be necessary to a choice. And if the House of Representatives shall not choose a President, whenever the right of choice shall devolve upon them, before the fourth day of March next following, then the Vice President shall act as President, as in the case of the death or other constitutional disability of the President. The person having the greatest number of votes as Vice President shall be the Vice President, if such number be a majority of the whole number of Electors appointed; and if no person have a majority, then from the two highest numbers on the list the Senate shall choose the Vice President; a quorum for the purpose shall consist of two-thirds of the whole number of Senators, and a majority of the whole number shall be necessary to a choice. But no person constitutionally ineligible to the office of President shall be eligible to that of Vice President of the United States.

Amendment XIII

Abolition of Slavery

The thirteenth amendment, adopted by the thirty-eighth Congress, held in 1865, was ratified by twenty-seven of the thirty-six States, and made a part of the Constitution, December 18, 1865.

Section 1. Neither slavery nor involuntary servitude,

In 1789, in New York City, George Washington took his oath as first President of the United States.

except as a punishment for crime whereof the party shall have been duly convicted, shall exist within the United States, or any place subject to their jurisdiction.

SECTION 2. Congress shall have power to enforce this article by appropriate legislation.

AMENDMENT XIV

Guarantee of Protection to All Citizens

The fourteenth amendment, adopted by the thirty-ninth Congress, held in 1866, was ratified by more than three-fourths of the States, and made a part of the Constitution, July 28, 1868.

SECTION 1. All persons born or naturalized in the United States, and subject to the jurisdiction thereof, are citizens of the United States and of the State wherein they reside. No State shall make or enforce any law which shall abridge the privileges or immunities of citizens of the United States; nor shall any State deprive any person of life, liberty, or property, without due process of law; nor deny to any person within its jurisdiction the equal protection of the laws.

Apportionment of Representatives

SECTION 2. Representatives shall be apportioned among the several States according to their respective numbers, counting the whole number of persons in each State, excluding Indians not taxed. But when the right to vote at any election for the choice of Electors for President and Vice President of the United States, Representatives in Congress, the executive and judicial officers of a State, or the members of the Legislature thereof, is denied to any of the male inhabitants of such State, being twenty-one years of age, and citizens of the United States, or in any way abridged, except for participation in rebellion, or other crime, the basis of representation therein shall be reduced in the proportion which the number of such male citizens shall bear to the whole number of male citizens twenty-one years of age in such State. (*See Article I, Section 2, paragraph 3, page 8.*)

Denial of Rights to Hold Public Office

SECTION 3. No person shall be a Senator or Representative in Congress, or Elector of President and Vice President, or hold any office, civil or military, under the United States, or under any State, who, having previously taken an oath, as a member of Congress, or as an officer of the United States, or as a member of any State Legislature, or as an executive or judicial officer of any State, to support the Constitution of the United States, shall have engaged in insurrection or rebellion against the same, or given aid or comfort to the enemies thereof. But Congress may, by a vote of two-thirds of each House, remove such disability.

Public Debts

SECTION 4. The validity of the public debt of the United States, authorized by law, including debts incurred for payment of pensions and bounties for services in suppressing insurrection or rebellion, shall not be questioned. But neither the United States nor any State shall assume or pay any debt or obligation incurred in aid of insurrection or rebellion against the United States, or any claim for the loss or emancipation of any slave; but all such debts, obligations, and claims shall be held illegal and void.

SECTION 5. The Congress shall have power to enforce, by appropriate legislation, the provisions of this article.

AMENDMENT XV

Suffrage Not Denied Because of Race, Color, or Servitude
The fifteenth amendment, adopted by the fortieth Congress, held

in 1869, was ratified by twenty-nine of the thirty-seven States then in the Union, and made a part of the Constitution, March 30, 1870.

SECTION 1.   The right of citizens of the United States to vote shall not be denied or abridged by the United States or by any State on account of race, color, or previous condition of servitude.

SECTION 2.   The Congress shall have power to enforce this article by appropriate legislation.

AMENDMENT XVI

Power to Levy Income Taxes

The sixteenth amendment, adopted by the sixty-first Congress, held in 1909, was ratified by thirty-eight of the forty-eight States, and made a part of the Constitution, February 25, 1913.

The Congress shall have power to lay and collect taxes on incomes, from whatever source derived, without apportionment among the several States, and without regard to any census or enumeration.

AMENDMENT XVII

Election of Senators by Direct Vote

The seventeenth amendment, adopted by the sixty-second Congress, held in 1912, was ratified by thirty-six States, and made a part of the Constitution, May 31, 1913.   This amendment was proposed to replace paragraphs 1 and 2, Section 3, Article I.

The Senate of the United States shall be composed of two Senators from each State, elected by the people thereof, for six years; and each Senator shall have one vote.   The electors in each State shall have the qualifications requisite for electors of the most numerous branch of the State Legislatures.

When vacancies happen in the representation of any State in the Senate, the executive authority of such State shall issue writs of election to fill such vacancies: *Provided,*

That the Legislature of any State may empower the Executive thereof to make temporary appointments until the people fill the vacancies by election as the Legislature may direct.

This amendment shall not be so construed as to affect the election or term of any Senator chosen before it becomes valid as part of the Constitution.

AMENDMENT XVIII

Prohibition of Manufacture and Sale of Liquor

The eighteenth amendment, adopted by the sixty-fifth Congress, held in 1917, was ratified by three-fourths of the States, and made a part of the Constitution, January 29, 1919. (See page 40.)

SECTION 1. After one year from the ratification of this article the manufacture, sale, or transportation of intoxicating liquors within, the importation thereof into, or the exportation thereof from the United States and all territory subject to the jurisdiction thereof for beverage purposes is hereby prohibited.

SECTION 2. The Congress and the several States shall have concurrent power to enforce this article by appropriate legislation.

SECTION 3. This article shall be inoperative unless it shall have been ratified as an amendment to the Constitution by the Legislatures of the several States, as provided in the Constitution, within seven years from the date of the submission hereof to the States by the Congress.

AMENDMENT XIX

Suffrage Rights Granted to Women

The nineteenth amendment, adopted by the sixty-sixth Congress, held in 1919, was ratified by three-fourths of the whole number of States, and made a part of the Constitution, August 26, 1920.

The right of the citizens of the United States to vote

shall not be denied or abridged by the United States or by any State on account of sex.

Congress shall have power to enforce this article by appropriate legislation.

AMENDMENT XX

Terms of Office of President, Vice President; Time Congress Shall Assemble

The twentieth amendment, adopted by the seventy-second Congress, held in 1932, was ratified by thirty-nine States, and made a part of the Constitution, February 6, 1933.

SECTION 1. The terms of the President and Vice President shall end at noon on the 20th day of January, and the terms of Senators and Representatives at noon on the 3d day of January, of the years in which such terms would have ended if this article had not been ratified; and the terms of their successors shall then begin.

SECTION 2. The Congress shall assemble at least once in every year, and such meeting shall begin at noon on the 3d day of January, unless they shall by law appoint a different day.

SECTION 3. If, at the time fixed for the beginning of the term of the President, the President elect shall have died, the Vice President elect shall become President. If a President shall not have been chosen before the time fixed for the beginning of his term, or if the President elect shall have failed to qualify, then the Vice President elect shall act as President until a President shall have qualified; and the Congress may by law provide for the case wherein neither a President elect nor a Vice President elect shall have qualified, declaring who shall then act as President, or the manner in which one who is to act shall be selected, and such person shall act accordingly until a President or Vice President shall have qualified.

Section 4. The Congress may by law provide for the case of the death of any of the persons from whom the House of Representatives may choose a President, whenever the right of choice shall have devolved upon them, and for the case of the death of any of the persons from whom the Senate may choose a Vice President whenever the right of choice shall have devolved upon them.

Section 5. Sections 1 and 2 shall take effect on the 15th day of October following the ratification of this article.

Section 6. This article shall be inoperative unless it shall have been ratified as an amendment to the Constitution by the Legislatures of three-fourths of the several States within seven years from the date of its submission.

Amendment XXI

Repeal of Prohibition

The twenty-first amendment, adopted by the seventy-second Congress, held in 1933, was ratified by thirty-six States, and made a part of the Constitution, December 5, 1933. (See page 38.)

Section 1. The eighteenth article of amendment to the Constitution of the United States is hereby repealed.

Section 2. The transportation or importation into any State, Territory, or possession of the United States for delivery or use therein of intoxicating liquors, in violation of the laws thereof, is hereby prohibited.

Section 3. This article shall be inoperative unless it shall have been ratified as an amendment to the Constitution by conventions in the several States, as provided in the Constitution, within seven years from the date of the submission hereof to the States by the Congress.

Amendment XXII

Term of the President Limited

The twenty-second amendment, adopted by the eighty-second congress, held in 1951, was ratified by more than three-fourths of the States and made a part of the Constitution March 1, 1951.

SECTION 1. No person shall be elected to the office of the President more than twice, and no person who has held the office of President, or acted as President, for more than two years of a term to which some other person was elected President shall be elected to the office of the President more than once. But this article shall not apply to any person holding the office of President when this article was proposed by the Congress, and shall not prevent any person who may be holding the office of President, or acting as President, during the term within which this article becomes operative from holding the office of President or acting as President during the remainder of such term.

SECTION 2. This article shall be inoperative unless it shall have been ratified as an amendment to the Constitution by the legislatures of three-fourths of the several states within seven years from the day of its submission to the states by the Congress.

Amendment XXIII

Presidential Vote for District of Columbia

The twenty-third amendment, adopted by the eighty-seventh Congress, held in 1960, was ratified by the required thirty-eight states and made a part of the Constitution April 3, 1961.

SECTION 1. The District constituting the seat of Government of the United States shall appoint in such manner as the Congress may direct:

A number of electors of President and Vice President equal to the whole number of Senators and Representatives in

Congress to which the District would be entitled if it were a State, but in no event more than the least populous State; they shall be in addition to those appointed by the States, but they shall be considered, for the purposes of the election of President and Vice President, to be electors appointed by a State; and they shall meet in the District and perform such duties as provided by the twelfth article of amendment.

SECTION 2.   The Congress shall have power to enforce this article by appropriate legislation.

AMENDMENT XXIV

Barring Poll Tax in Federal Elections

The twenty-fourth amendment, adopted by the eighty-seventh Congress, held in 1962, was ratified by the required thirty-eight states and made a part of the Constitution on January 23, 1964.

SECTION 1.   The right of citizens of the United States to vote in any primary or other election for President or Vice President, for electors for President or Vice President, or for Senator or Representative in Congress, shall not be denied or abridged by the United States or any State by reason of failure to pay any poll tax or other tax.

SECTION 2.   The Congress shall have the power to enforce this article by appropriate legislation.

AMENDMENT XXV

Presidential Disability and Vice-Presidential Vacancies

The twenty-fifth amendment, adopted by the eighty-eighth Congress, held in 1964, was ratified by the required thirty-eight states and made a part of the Constitution on February 10, 1967.

SECTION 1.   In case of the removal of the President from

office or his death or resignation, the Vice President shall become President.

SECTION 2. Whenever there is a vacancy in the office of the Vice President, the President shall nominate a Vice President who shall take the office upon confirmation by a majority vote of both houses of Congress.

SECTION 3. Whenever the President transmits to the President pro tempore of the Senate and the Speaker of the House of Representatives his written declaration that he is unable to discharge the powers and duties of his office, and until he transmits to them a written declaration to the contrary, such powers and duties shall be discharged by the Vice President as Acting President.

SECTION 4. Whenever the Vice President and a majority of either the principal officers of the executive departments, or of such other body as Congress may by law provide, transmit to the President pro tempore of the Senate and the Speaker of the House of Representatives their written declaration that the President is unable to discharge the powers and duties of his office, the Vice President shall immediately assume the powers and duties of the office as Acting President.

Thereafter, when the President transmits to the President pro tempore of the Senate and the Speaker of the House of Representatives his written declaration that no inability exists, he shall resume the powers and duties of his office unless the Vice President and a majority of either the principal officer of the executive department, or of such other body as Congress may by law provide, transmit within four days to the President pro tempore of the Senate and the Speaker of the House of Representatives their written declaration that the President is unable to discharge the powers and duties of his office. Thereupon Congress shall decide the issue, assembling within 48 hours for that purpose if not in session. If the Congress, within 21 days after receipt of the latter written declaration, or, if Congress is not in session, within 21 days after Congress is required to assemble, determines by two-thirds vote of both houses that the President is unable to discharge the powers and duties of his office, the Vice President shall continue to discharge the same as Acting President; otherwise, the President shall resume the powers and duties of his office.

Amendment XXVI

Suffrage Rights Granted to Persons Age 18

The twenty-sixth amendment, adopted by the ninety-third Congress, held in 1971, was ratified by the required thirty-eight states and made a part of the Constitution on June 30, 1971.

SECTION 1.   The right of citizens of the United States, who are eighteen years or older, to vote shall not be denied or abridged by the United States or by any State on account of age.

SECTION 2.   The Congress shall have the power to enforce this article by appropriate legislation.

Amendment XXVII

Compensation for Services of Senators and Representatives

Congress submitted the text of the twenty-seventh amendment to the States as part of the proposed Bill of Rights on September 25, 1789. The Amendment was not ratified together with the first ten Amendments, which became effective on December 15, 1791. The twenty-seventh Amendment was ratified on May 7, 1992, by the vote of Michigan.

No law, varying the compensation for the services of the Senators and Representatives, shall take effect until an election of Representatives shall have intervened.

THE MAKING OF THE CONSTITUTION

The Declaration of Independence marked the birth of a new nation, but its survival was not well assured until the ratification of the Constitution. Before the adoption of the Constitution, the United States had a very weak central government. The Second Continental Congress held the thirteen States together in a semblance of unity for the first six years of the Revolution.

In March, 1781, the "Articles of Confederation and perpetual Union" went into effect, but despite their high-sounding title, they left much to be desired. The will or whim of even one of the sovereign States might have dissolved this "league of friendship" at any time during its eight years of precarious existence. There was neither an effective Executive nor a Supreme Court. The enactment of important legislation required the assent of at least nine of the State delegations in Congress, and this body sometimes had no quorum for weeks at a time. With no power of taxation, the central government was dependent upon the States for funds. Lacking an adequate army and navy, and harmony between the jealous States, the migratory Congress was not accorded respect at home or abroad. The newly gained liberty sometimes degenerated into license, and the hard-won gains of the Revolution were in danger of being lost.

Little wonder, then, that Washington, Hamilton, and other leading patriots early urged that the central government should be strengthened. At Madison's suggestion, commissioners from Maryland and Virginia met at Mt. Vernon in 1785, and settled several long-standing differences between those two States. Cheered by this success, a general convention, to discuss matters relating to trade, was called to assemble at Annapolis in May, 1786. Poor attendance defeated the purpose of the meeting, but the delegates recommended that representatives from all of the States should be called together in order to strengthen the Confederation. Congress set May 14, 1787, and Independence Hall, Philadelphia, as the date and place of this meeting.

The fifty-five delegates who attended the Convention included many men of outstanding ability and service. Eight had signed the Declaration of Independence; seven had served as Governors of States; twenty-one had fought in the Revolution; and thirty-nine had been in Congress. Several held degrees from British universities, and others were graduates of Yale, King's, Harvard, Princeton, or William and Mary College. Those leaders, however, who had been most conspicuous for their radicalism in the early days of the Revolution were not present.

Among the members was the wise, snowy-haired Franklin, perhaps the greatest American then living, and honored by many of the learned societies of Europe. There was John Dickinson of Delaware, whose patriotism in the dark days of the war had amply atoned for his refusal to sign the Declaration of Independence. He, James Wilson of Pennsylvania, and John Rutledge of South Carolina, also in the Convention, were three of the best lawyers of America. The keen-minded Alexander Hamilton of New York was there; so too were Gouverneur Morris of Pennsylvania, a master with his pen; the young and brilliant Charles Pinckney of South Carolina; and Edmund Randolph, the Governor of Virginia. Perhaps the Constitution reflects most largely the influence of James Madison. He and Randolph persuaded Washington to attend the Convention. The revered General was escorted into Philadelphia on May 13 by the City Light Horse Troop while the church bells pealed a welcome. Robert Morris, the financier of the Revolution and also a member of the Convention, was his host.

Owing to bad weather and roads, lack of funds, and other causes, it was May 25 before enough delegates reached Philadelphia to make a quorum. Washington was then unanimously elected to the presidency of the Convention. Without much debate, the members decided to frame an entirely new Constitution rather than merely to propose amendments to the Articles of Confederation. From the outset, however, a serious cleavage opened between the spokesmen of the big and little States. This division was not primarily on the subject of the fields of power to be granted to the central government, but rather on the apportionment among the States of taxes and representation in Congress, and on the method whereby the delegated powers could be enforced. The deputies from the large States rallied about the so-called Virginia Plan, framed by Madison and others before the Convention first convened, and introduced by Randolph on May 29. For two weeks thereafter the details of this plan were the leading subjects of debate, and mid-June arrived before the delegates from the small States introduced their counter-proposal known as the New Jersey Plan.

The Convention deadlocked time and again on critical

questions, and occasionally the members seemed ready to go home in despair. Hamilton believed that the people were "tired of an excess of democracy," that the State Governors should be appointed by the central government, and that the national Executive and the Senators should be elected during good behavior for life. At the other extreme were those who still urged that the Articles of Confederation, if amended, would be adequate. In view of so many conflicting viewpoints, it becomes understandable why Franklin should move on June 28 that "we have prayers every morning."

Under these circumstances, mutual concessions had to be made. Of these, the "Connecticut Compromise," concerning the structure of Congress, is probably the best known, but in truth the entire Constitution is a bundle of compromises between the views of those members who wished the central government to operate only through the State governments, and those who urged that it rest wholly upon the people themselves.

By early September, the work of the Convention was sufficiently near completion to warrant the appointment of a Committee on Style and Arrangement. Of the five members of this Committee, Gouverneur Morris was the chief. The phraseology of the Constitution owes much to his facile pen. The revised draft was submitted to the Convention on September 12, and five days later, thirty-nine members signed the completed document. "It . . . astonishes me, Sir," said the venerable Franklin on that day, "to find this system approaching so near to perfection as it does; . . . I hope therefore that for our own sakes . . . and for the sake of posterity, we shall act heartily and unanimously in recommending this Constitution . . . wherever our influence may extend, and turn our future thoughts and endeavors to the means of having it well administered."

Despite Franklin's sage advice, some of the delegates worked with might and main to prevent the ratification of the Constitution. Because of the heated opposition, almost three years went by before the last of the thirteen States gave its assent. But the Constitution provided that it should go into effect after nine States had approved. New Hampshire's ratification on June 21, 1788, completed this quota, and shortly thereafter the Congress of the Confederation took the necessary steps to launch the new government and to prepare for its own demise.

On the evening of March 3, 1789, the big guns on the New York Battery fired a parting salute to the old Confederacy. The following day the new Union was similarly ushered in with the thunder of cannon and the ringing of church bells. On April 30, George Washington was escorted amid great acclaim to Federal Hall at the corner of Broad and Wall streets, New York City, and was there inaugurated as the first President of the United States.

For more than two centuries, the Constitution has stood as a guardian of individual liberty and the supreme law of the land.

The Liberty Bell cracked on July 8, 1835, when it was tolled upon the death of Chief Justice Marshall.

THE WRITING
OF THE DECLARATION
OF INDEPENDENCE

It was June, 1776. The battles of Lexington and Concord had been fought, and the colonies were actually at war with Great Britain. The Second Continental Congress was assembled in Philadelphia. On June 7, Richard Henry Lee, of Virginia, moved Congress that "these United Colonies are, and of right ought to be, free and independent States, . . . absolved from all allegiance to the British Crown." John Adams seconded the motion, but some delegates hesitated to take so irrevocable a step, and this resolution was not adopted until July 2.

In the meantime, Congress appointed a committee to prepare a statement justifying the action about to be taken. Its report, largely the work of Thomas Jefferson, was vigorously debated in Congress before it was adopted in somewhat altered form on July 4. This was our Declaration of Independence, although the passage of Lee's motion, two days earlier, really marked the beginning of the independence of the United States. The Liberty Bell did not ring on the nation's birthday.

Most of the signatures on the Declaration were affixed on August 2, 1776. About fifteen of them were added later in that year.

Keystone View Co.

The five members of the Declaration Committee — Benjamin Franklin, Thomas Jefferson, Robert R. Livingston, John Adams, and Roger Sherman

THE DECLARATION OF INDEPENDENCE

In Congress, July 4, 1776

The Unanimous Declaration of the Thirteen United States of America

PREAMBLE

WHEN, in the course of human events, it becomes necessary for one people to dissolve the political bands which have connected them with another, and to assume among the powers of the earth the separate and equal station to which the laws of nature and of nature's God entitle them, a decent respect to the opinions of mankind requires that they should declare the causes which impel them to the separation.

We hold these truths to be self-evident: That all men are created equal; that they are endowed by their Creator with certain unalienable rights; that among these are life, liberty, and the pursuit of happiness; that, to secure these rights, governments are instituted among men, deriving their just powers from the consent of the governed; that whenever any form of government becomes destructive of these ends, it is the right of the people to alter or to abolish it and to institute new government, laying its foundation on such principles, and organizing its powers in such form, as to them shall seem most likely to effect their safety and happiness. Prudence, indeed, will dictate that governments long established should not be changed for light and transient causes; and, accordingly, all experience hath shown that mankind are more disposed to suffer while evils are sufferable, than to right themselves by abolishing the forms to which they are accustomed. But when a long train of abuses and usurpations, pursuing invariably the same object, evinces a design to reduce them under absolute despotism, it is their right, it is their duty, to throw off such government and to provide new guards for their future security. Such has been the patient sufferance of these colonies; and such is now the necessity which constrains them to alter their former systems of government.

Specific Charges against the King

The history of the present King of Great Britain is a history of repeated injuries and usurpations, all having in direct object the establishment of an absolute tyranny over these States. To prove this, let facts be submitted to a candid world:

He has refused his assent to laws, the most wholesome and necessary for the public good.

He has forbidden his Governors to pass laws of immediate and pressing importance, unless suspended in their operation till his assent should be obtained; and, when so suspended, he has utterly neglected to attend to them.

He has refused to pass other laws for the accommodation of large districts of people, unless those people would relinquish the right of representation in the Legislature, a right inestimable to them and formidable to tyrants only.

He has called together legislative bodies at places unusual, uncomfortable, and distant from the depository of their public records, for the sole purpose of fatiguing them into compliance with his measures.

He has dissolved representative Houses repeatedly for opposing with manly firmness his invasions on the rights of the people.

He has refused for a long time after such dissolutions to cause others to be elected; whereby the legislative powers, incapable of annihilation, have returned to the people at large for their exercise; the State remaining, in the meantime, exposed to all the dangers of invasions from without and convulsions within.

He has endeavored to prevent the population of these States; for that purpose obstructing the laws for naturalization of foreigners, refusing to pass others to encourage their migration hither, and raising the conditions of new appropriations of lands.

He has obstructed the administration of justice by refusing his assent to laws for establishing judiciary powers.

He has made judges dependent on his will alone for the tenure of their offices and the amount and payment of their salaries.

He has erected a multitude of new offices, and sent hither swarms of officers to harass our people and eat out their substance.

He has kept among us, in times of peace, standing armies, without the consent of our Legislatures.

He has affected to render the military independent of, and superior to, the civil power.

He has combined with others to subject us to a jurisdiction foreign to our Constitution and unacknowledged by our laws, giving his assent to their acts of pretended legislation:

For quartering large bodies of armed troops among us;

For protecting them, by a mock trial, from punishment for any murders which they should commit on the inhabitants of these States;

For cutting off our trade with all parts of the world;

For imposing taxes on us without our consent;

For depriving us, in many cases, of the benefits of trial by jury;

For transporting us beyond seas to be tried for pretended offenses;

For abolishing the free system of English laws in a neighboring province, establishing therein an arbitrary government, and enlarging its boundaries so as to render it at once an example and fit instrument for introducing the same absolute rule into these colonies;

For taking away our charters, abolishing our most valuable laws, and altering fundamentally the forms of our governments;

For suspending our own Legislatures, and declaring themselves invested with power to legislate for us in all cases whatsoever.

He has abdicated government here by declaring us out of his protection and waging war against us.

He has plundered our seas, ravaged our coasts, burnt our towns, and destroyed the lives of our people.

He is at this time transporting large armies of foreign mercenaries to complete the works of death, desolation, and tyranny, already begun with circumstances of cruelty

In this room in Independence Hall the Declaration of Independence was adopted.

and perfidy scarcely paralleled in the most barbarous ages, and totally unworthy the head of a civilized nation.

He has constrained our fellow citizens, taken captive on the high seas, to bear arms against their country, to become the executioners of their friends and brethren, or to fall themselves by their hands.

He has excited domestic insurrections amongst us, and has endeavored to bring on the inhabitants of our frontiers the merciless Indian savages, whose known rule of warfare is an undistinguished destruction of all ages, sexes, and conditions.

In every stage of these oppressions we have petitioned for redress in the most humble terms: our repeated petitions have been answered only by repeated injury. A prince, whose character is thus marked by every act which may define a tyrant, is unfit to be the ruler of a free people.

Nor have we been wanting in attentions to our British brethren. We have warned them from time to time of attempts by their Legislature to extend an unwarrantable jurisdiction over us. We have reminded them of the circumstances of our emigration and settlement here. We have appealed to their native justice and magnanimity, and we have conjured them by the ties of our common kindred to disavow these usurpations which would inevitably interrupt our connections and correspondence. They, too, have been deaf to the voice of justice and of consanguinity. We must, therefore, acquiesce in the necessity which denounces our separation, and hold them, as we hold the rest of mankind, enemies in war; in peace, friends.

Conclusion and Declaration

WE, THEREFORE, THE REPRESENTATIVES OF THE UNITED

This facsimile of the Declaration of Independence was made from a photograph of the original document, now in the Library of Congress.

STATES OF AMERICA, in General Congress assembled, appealing to the Supreme Judge of the world for the rectitude of our intentions, do, in the name and by the authority of the good people of these colonies, solemnly publish and declare that these United Colonies are, and of right ought to be, FREE AND INDEPENDENT STATES; that they are absolved from all allegiance to the British Crown, and that all political connection between them and the State of Great Britain is, and ought to be, totally dissolved; and that as free and independent states they have full power to levy war, conclude peace, contract alliances, establish commerce, and to do all other acts and things which independent States may of right do. And for the support of this declaration, with a firm reliance on the protection of Divine Providence, we mutually pledge to each other our lives, our fortunes, and our sacred honor.

JOHN HANCOCK

New Hampshire
JOSIAH BARTLETT
WM. WHIPPLE
MATTHEW THORNTON

Massachusetts Bay
SAML. ADAMS
JOHN ADAMS
ROBT. TREAT PAINE
ELBRIDGE GERRY

Rhode Island
STEP. HOPKINS
WILLIAM ELLERY

Connecticut
ROGER SHERMAN

Connecticut (continued)
SAM'EL HUNTINGTON
WM. WILLIAMS
OLIVER WOLCOTT

New York
WM. FLOYD
PHIL. LIVINGSTON
FRANS. LEWIS
LEWIS MORRIS

New Jersey
RICHD. STOCKTON
JNO. WITHERSPOON
FRAS. HOPKINSON
JOHN HART
ABRA. CLARK

Pennsylvania

Robt. Morris
Benjamin Rush
Benja. Franklin
John Morton
Geo. Clymer
Jas. Smith
Geo. Taylor
James Wilson
Geo. Ross

Delaware

Caesar Rodney
Geo. Read
Tho. M'Kean

Maryland

Samuel Chase
Wm. Paca
Thos. Stone
Charles Carroll of
  Carrollton

Virginia

George Wythe
Richard Henry Lee
Th. Jefferson
Benja. Harrison
Thos. Nelson, Jr.
Francis Lightfoot Lee
Carter Braxton

North Carolina

Wm Hooper
Joseph Hewes
John Penn

South Carolina

Edward Rutledge
Thos. Heyward, Junr
Thomas Lynch, Junr
Arthur Middleton

Georgia

Button Gwinnett
Lyman Hall
Geo. Walton

Abraham Lincoln, delivering his address at Gettysburg, Pennsylvania, on
November 19, 1863

LINCOLN'S
GETTYSBURG ADDRESS

The several copies of this address, made at the time, vary considerably in detail. This one follows "Lincoln's first revision."

Four score and seven years ago our fathers brought forth upon this continent, a new nation, conceived in Liberty, and dedicated to the proposition that all men are created equal. Now we are engaged in a great civil war, testing whether that nation, or any nation so conceived, and so dedicated, can long endure. We are met on a great battlefield of that war. We have come to dedicate a portion of that field, as a final resting place for those who here gave their lives, that that nation might live. It is altogether fitting and proper that we should do this. But, in a larger sense, we cannot dedicate—we cannot consecrate—we cannot hallow—this ground. The brave men, living and dead, who struggled here, have consecrated it, far above our poor power to add or detract. The world will little note, nor long remember, what we say here, but it can never forget what they did here. It is for us, the living, rather, to be dedicated here to the unfinished work which they who fought here, have, thus far, so nobly advanced. It is rather for us to be here dedicated to the great task remaining before us—that from these honored dead we take increased devotion to that cause for which they here gave the last full measure of devotion—that we here highly resolve that these dead shall not have died in vain—that this nation, under God, shall have a new birth of freedom—and that, government of the people, by the people, for the people, shall not perish from the earth.

Dates on which the Original Thirteen States Ratified the Constitution

Delaware......Dec. 7, 1787   Maryland....April 28, 1788
Pennsylvania..Dec. 12, 1787   So. Carolina...May 23, 1788
New Jersey...Dec. 18, 1787   New HampshireJune 21,1788
Georgia........Jan. 2, 1788   Virginia......June 25, 1788
Connecticut....Jan. 9, 1788   New York.....July 26, 1788
Massachusetts..Feb. 6, 1788   No. Carolina..Nov. 21, 1789

Rhode Island..May 29, 1790

Dates on which States Have Been Admitted to the Union since 1790

Vermont.....March 4, 1791   Minnesota....May 11, 1858
Kentucky......June 1, 1792   Oregon.......Feb. 14, 1859
Tennessee......June 1, 1796   Kansas........Jan. 29, 1861
Ohio.........March 1, 1803   West Virginia June 20, 1863
Louisiana.....April 30, 1812   Nevada.......Oct. 31, 1864
Indiana.......Dec. 11, 1816   Nebraska....March 1, 1867
Mississippi....Dec. 10, 1817   Colorado.......Aug. 1, 1876
Illinois.........Dec. 3, 1818   North Dakota..Nov. 2, 1889
Alabama......Dec. 14, 1819   South Dakota..Nov. 2, 1889
Maine......March 15, 1820   Montana......Nov. 8, 1889
Missouri....August 10, 1821   Washington...Nov. 11, 1889
Arkansas.....June 15, 1836   Idaho..........July 3, 1890
Michigan......Jan. 26, 1837   Wyoming.....July 10, 1890
Florida   ...March 3, 1845   Utah..........Jan. 4, 1896
Texas........Dec. 29, 1845   Oklahoma...Nov. 16, 1907
Iowa.........Dec. 28, 1846   New Mexico....Jan. 6, 1912
Wisconsin.....May 29, 1848   Arizona.......Feb. 14, 1912
California.....Sept. 9, 1850   Alaska.........Jan. 3, 1959

Hawaii..Aug. 21, 1959

PART II

The Flag

OF OUR UNITED STATES

By *Colonel James A. Moss*

Late President General, the United States Flag Association

Acknowledgment is made to the
Standard Printing and Publishing Co.,
Huntington, West Virginia,
for the use of the illustrations
on pp. 72–81, from *Flags of America*
by Colonel William H. Waldron.

CONTENTS

WHAT THE FLAG MEANS

CHARLES EVANS HUGHES

This Flag means more than association and reward. It is the symbol of our national unity, our national endeavor, our national aspiration. It tells you of the struggle for independence, of union preserved, of liberty and union one and inseparable, of the sacrifices of brave men and women to whom the ideals and honor of this nation have been dearer than life.

It means America first; it means an undivided allegiance. It means America united, strong and efficient, equal to her tasks. It means that you cannot be saved by the valor and devotion of your ancestors; that to each generation comes its patriotic duty; and that upon your willingness to sacrifice and endure as those before you have sacrificed and endured rests the national hope.

It speaks of equal rights; of the inspiration of free institutions exemplified and vindicated; of liberty under law intelligently conceived and impartially administered.

There is not a thread in it but scorns self-indulgence, weakness, and rapacity. It is eloquent of our community interests, outweighing all divergencies of opinion, and of our common destiny.

(From a speech delivered in 1916.)

The original Star-Spangled Banner that flew over Fort McHenry during the bombardment on the night of September 13–14, 1814, and inspired Francis Scott Key to write our National Anthem. The Flag, 30 by 34 feet, is now in the Smithsonian Institution, Washington, D.C.

HISTORY OF THE FLAG

The flag of a people symbolizes their hopes and aspirations, their struggles and sacrifices, their joys and achievements. If these be fine and noble, their flag is great, but if their aspirations, conduct, and accomplishments be ignoble, then their flag means little or nothing. In other words, the flag of a country is what its people make it. It is nothing more, nothing less.

Those who founded this nation of ours, through their aspirations, struggles, sacrifices, and achievements, made and handed down to us a great country with a great Flag, symbolizing ideals and institutions which, in a little over two centuries, have made the United States a nation second to none in greatness and power, wealth and influence.

In order to understand properly the history of the Flag of the United States — its origin and evolution — it is necessary to know about the principal flags of other countries which have influenced its design. Especially should we be familiar with the development of the flag of Great Britain, which no doubt had greater influence on the design of the United States national emblem than any other flag.

THE FLAGS OF GREAT BRITAIN

CROSS OF ST. ANDREW

One of the earliest flags of Great Britain to have a possible influence on the Flag of the United States was the Cross of St. Andrew. From about the middle of the eighth century the Cross of St. Andrew, Scotland's patron saint, had been the national standard of that country. It was a white diagonal cross on a blue field, thus containing two of the colors of our present Flag. The Cross of St. Andrew was brought to America by the Scots during their early explora-

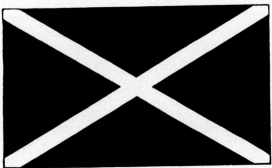

Cross of St. Andrew

tions and settlements in Nova Scotia at the time of the English settlements at Plymouth, Massachusetts, and Jamestown, Virginia.

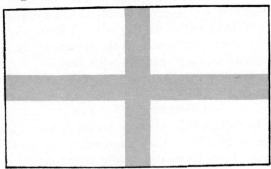

Cross of St. George

CROSS OF ST. GEORGE

Another early flag of Great Britain of interest to us is the

Cross of St. George — a red cross on a white field. It was in the latter part of the thirteenth century that Edward I of

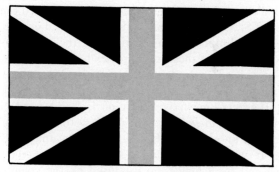

Union Jack—The King's Colors

England became so interested in the story of St. George and the dragon that he adopted the Cross of St. George as the flag of England. This flag was first unfurled in North

Meteor Flag—Red Ensign

America in 1497, by John Cabot, who probably landed on the coast of Newfoundland.

UNION JACK — THE KING'S COLORS

In 1606, James VI of Scotland, who three years before had ascended the throne of England as James I, decreed that the Crosses of St. George and St. Andrew be united on one field to typify the linking of the destinies of the two countries. The combination of these two Crosses brought together the colors of red, white, and blue, which almost two centuries later became our national colors. In time the new flag of James I became known as the Union Jack, the word "Jack" being derived from *Jacques*, the French word for James. The flag was also known as the Grand Union Flag and the King's Colors. It was the flag under which England colonized America and for a long time was used by the colonists. It flew from the mainmasts of the "Constant," which brought the English settlers to Jamestown in 1607, and of the "Mayflower," which brought the Pilgrims to Plymouth in 1620, while the Cross of St. George was displayed from the foremasts of these vessels.

METEOR FLAG — RED ENSIGN

In 1707 a flag consisting of a red field* and the King's Colors as a canton was adopted as the national standard of Great Britain, and as such was well known to early American colonists. This Meteor Flag of England, as it was sometimes called, was also known as the British Red Ensign and continued to be the national flag of Great Britain until 1801. It was the flag of Great Britain in America throughout the War of the Revolution and the banner under which Cornwallis surrendered at Yorktown, October 19, 1781.

*A Glossary of Flag Terms may be found on p. 126.

DUTCH FLAGS

While there is reason to believe that the British flags had the greatest influence in determining the design and colors of the Flag of the United States, it is probable that an influence was exerted also by the flags of the Dutch Republic, the United States of Netherlands, and the Dutch West India Company. For half a century before the English began colonizing the Middle Atlantic states, the Dutch had been settling and governing New Netherland, which consisted of the Dutch settlements in New York, New Jersey, Pennsylvania, and Delaware. So the Dutch flags with their dominant stripes and colors of red, white, and blue had been familiar to American colonists for over a hundred years. Incidentally, it may be noted that the word "stripe," so essential a part of our Flag vocabulary, is from the Dutch *strijpe*, "a stripe, streak."

COLONIAL FLAGS

Before the Continental Congress adopted a flag for the United States, in 1777, various banners of different designs were used in a number of the colonies. Those here mentioned were among the best known and most interesting.

TAUNTON FLAG

In 1774, two years before the signing of the Declaration of Independence, the so-called Taunton Flag was unfurled at Taunton, Massachusetts. It was, in reality, the Meteor Flag of England, with the word "Liberty" across the lower part of the red field.

BEDFORD FLAG

The Bedford Flag, which waved over the "embattled

farmers" at Concord, April 19, 1775, when they fired "the shot heard round the world," is considered by many to exceed

Taunton Flag

all other Colonial flags both in interest and in historic value. This famous standard is today carefully preserved in the

Bedford Flag

Public Library of Bedford, Massachusetts. A mailed arm extends from a cloud, the hand clasping a sword. A scroll

76

bears the motto, *Vince aut Morire* ("Conquer or Die"). The three disks are supposed to represent cannon balls.

Moultrie Liberty Flag

To this flag belongs the honor of being the first flag of the American Revolution to receive a baptism of British fire.

Bunker Hill Flag

MOULTRIE FLAG

This flag is said to have been the earliest displayed in the

South (1775). It was a blue flag with a white crescent in its upper left-hand corner. A year later the word "Liberty" was emblazoned on it.

The story of the Moultrie Flag's origin is interesting. When Colonel William Moultrie occupied Fort Johnson, on James Island, in September, 1775, his troops wore a blue uniform, with a silver crescent on the cap. Realizing that a flag was necessary, he improvised one having a blue field, with a white crescent in the canton. This was the flag that Sergeant Jasper so gallantly rescued on June 28, 1776, when the British fleet attacked Fort Sullivan at Charleston, South Carolina. For his gallantry the Governor presented him with his own sword and offered him a Lieutenant's commission, but the Sergeant, who could neither read nor write, declined the promotion, saying, "Sir, I am not fit to keep the company of officers."

PINE TREE FLAGS

Pine Tree Flags of different designs were very popular in New England, the pine tree symbolizing the hardiness of the New Englanders. One form, known as the Bunker Hill Flag, consisted of a blue flag with a white canton bearing the red Cross of St. George and a green pine tree. Another form of the Pine Tree Flag—the one adopted by Massachusetts in 1776—had a white field with a pine tree in the center, above which were the words, "An Appeal to Heaven."

RATTLESNAKE FLAGS

Used especially in the South, the Rattlesnake Flag, in a variety of forms, rivaled in popularity the Pine Tree Flag. One form, known as the Gadsden Flag, had a yellow field with a coiled rattlesnake in the center, under which appeared the words, "Don't Tread on Me."

Various reasons are given why the rattlesnake symbol should have been selected. Benjamin Franklin is said to have defended the symbol on several grounds: that the rattlesnake is found only in North America; that among the ancients serpents were considered possessed of wisdom and vigilance; that the rattlesnake does not attack without first giving warning; and that the number of rattles increases with age — hence the symbol was especially appropriate for the anticipated growth of the United States.

RHODE ISLAND FLAG

Because of the oft repeated claim that the design of the union of the Flag of the United States was suggested by the stars in the flag of Rhode Island, this flag is one of the most interesting of the Colonial flags. It had the word "Hope" in a white field, and thirteen white stars in a blue canton. The middle vertical and horizontal lines of three stars form the Cross of St. George, while the two diagonal lines of five stars form the Cross of St. Andrew, but whether this occurred through coincidence or design is not known.

FIRST FLAG OF THE UNITED COLONIES

Variously designated as the Cambridge Flag, the Grand Union Flag, or the Great Union Flag, the first flag of the United Colonies was flown over George Washington's headquarters at Cambridge, Massachusetts, January 1, 1776. It had thirteen horizontal red and white stripes, with the combined Crosses of St. George and St. Andrew in a canton with a blue field (the King's Colors). In fact, it was the Meteor Flag of England, with the solid red field divided by white ribbons so as to make thirteen red

AN APPEAL TO HEAVEN

Pine Tree Flag

and white stripes, representing the thirteen rebelling colonies. This similarity may at first seem strange, but it must be borne in mind that at the time the idea of independence

DONT TREAD ON ME

Gadsden Flag

from England was not seriously considered by the colonists, so that the King's Colors in this flag showed the allegiance which the colonies felt they still owed to the mother country.

Rhode Island Flag

When Washington heard, for the first time, the Declaration of Independence in New York City, July 9, 1776, the Grand Union Flag was flown for the occasion. While the Army used

First Flag of the United Colonies

this flag over barracks, camps, and fortifications, it never, so far as is known, carried it in battle. In fact, it was short-lived, as it was naturally inappropriate and unpopular after the signing of the Declaration of Independence, July 4, 1776.

ADOPTION OF FLAG OF THE UNITED STATES

On June 14, 1777, the Continental Congress in Philadelphia adopted the following resolution:

Resolved, That the Flag of the United States be thirteen stripes, alternate red and white; that the union be thirteen stars, white in a blue field representing a new constellation.

The significant part of this resolution is the words, "Thirteen stars, white in a blue field representing a new constellation," for it is in them that we find the very soul and spirit of the American Flag. These were the words which, like scintillating stars in the heavens, signaled to the world the birth of the first nation on earth dedicated to the personal and religious liberty of mankind.

It will be noted that the resolution of adoption did not prescribe how the stars were to be arranged. As a result, in the beginning they were arranged in various ways, including a circle. Some say the circle was to indicate the equality of the states, while others contend it was to symbolize the hope that the Union would be without end.

TWO STARS AND TWO STRIPES ADDED

In 1791, the state of Vermont was admitted into the Union, and in 1792, Kentucky was admitted. The representatives of these two states in Congress wanted their states recognized in the Flag; so on January 13, 1794, Congress enacted a law to the effect that, beginning May 1, 1795, there should be fifteen stars and fifteen stripes in the Flag.

1777 June 14. Saturday June 14 1777

— Resolved That the Flag of the united states be thirteen stripes alternate red and white, that the Union be 13 stars white in a blue field representing a new constellation. —

The above is a facsimile of the original resolution passed by the Continental Congress, June 14, 1777, adopting the Flag of the United States. This was ten years before the adoption of the Constitution, September 17, 1787. The handwriting is that of Charles Thomson, secretary of the Continental Congress.

Note that "Flag" is spelled with a capital *F*, but "United States" is spelled with a small *u* and a small *s*. Note, also, the wording, "the Flag of the United States," which gives us the correct, official designation of our national emblem.

In some Flags the stars were staggered in five horizontal rows of three stars each, while in other Flags they were arranged in three horizontal rows of five stars each, one directly above the other. The Flag that flew over Fort McHenry when Francis Scott Key was inspired to write "The Star-Spangled Banner" had its stars staggered in five rows.

Thirteen Stripes — Star for Each State

In 1818, the number of states having increased to twenty, Congress passed a law (1) giving representation in the Flag to the five states—Tennessee (1796), Ohio (1802), Louisiana (1812), Indiana (1816), and Mississippi (1817)—that had been admitted into the Union after the last Flag Act had been adopted, thereby increasing the number of stars to twenty, effective July 4, 1818; (2) returning the number of stripes to the original thirteen; and (3) decreeing that thereafter a star should be added to the blue field for each new state admitted into the Union, such addition to take effect on the Fourth of July following the date of admission into the Union—that is, the law provided, in effect, "Every Star a State; Every State a Star."

Stars Tell Growth of Nation

It is in the stars of the Flag that we read the growth of the American nation. As the nation has grown in size, so have the stars in the Flag increased in number.

At Beginning of Mexican War

From the time the stars increased to twenty, in 1818, to the beginning of the Mexican War in 1846, Illinois (1818), Ala-

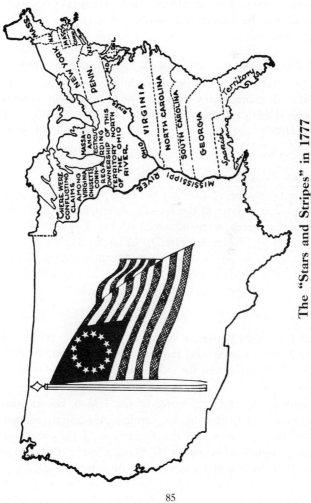

The "Stars and Stripes" in 1777

In this early Flag the stars in the blue field were arranged in the form of a circle to signify the hope that the Union would be without end; also, to symbolize the equality of the states.

bama (1819), Maine (1820), Missouri (1821), Arkansas (1836), Michigan (1837), Florida (1845), and Texas (1845) were admitted into the Union, the number of stars thus reaching twenty-eight.

At Beginning of the War Between the States

From 1846 until the beginning of the War between the States in 1861, six more states—Iowa (1846), Wisconsin (1848), California (1850), Minnesota (1858), Oregon (1859), and Kansas (1861)—were admitted, and the number of stars increased to thirty-four.

At Beginning of Spanish-American War

From the beginning of the War between the States in 1861 to the commencement of the Spanish-American War in 1898, eleven more states were admitted—West Virginia (1863), Nevada (1864), Nebraska (1867), Colorado (1876), North Dakota (1889), South Dakota (1889), Montana (1889), Washington (1889), Idaho (1890), Wyoming (1890), and Utah (1896)—making the number of stars forty-five.

Today

In 1907 Oklahoma became a state, and in 1912 the territories of New Mexico and Arizona reached their statehood. In 1959 Alaska and Hawaii voted for statehood, bringing the stars in the flag to fifty.

In addition to the fifty states of the Union, constituting the Continental United States, foreign possessions of such expanse have come under the protection of the Stars and Stripes, as indicated on pages 90–91, that today it may truly be said that the sun never sets on the American Flag.

The American Flag from 1795 to 1818

During these twenty-three years the Flag had fifteen stripes.

87

THE BETSY ROSS STORY

The distinction of having made the first American Flag is often given to Betsy Ross, a Philadelphia Quaker. According to the popular story, in June, 1776, shortly before the Declaration of Independence was signed, George Washington, George Ross, and Robert Morris called on Betsy Ross and told her that they, as a Committee of Congress, wanted her to make for them an American flag according to a sketch they had. She replied, "I don't know whether I can, but I'll try." After the Flag was completed, the Committee submitted it to Congress and it was unanimously adopted, thereby giving to Betsy Ross the honor of having made the first American Flag.

Almost without exception, however, historians assail the accuracy of the Betsy Ross Flag story, which is based entirely on family hearsay and is not supported in any way whatsoever by contemporary evidence. To quote the late Admiral George H. Preble, United States Navy, universally acknowledged as America's greatest Flag historian:

"It will probably never be known who designed our union of stars, the records of Congress being silent on the subject, and there being no mention or suggestion of it in any of the voluminous correspondence or diaries of the time, public or private, which have ever been published."

Like the George Washington cherry-tree legend, the Betsy Ross Flag story is intriguing. It appeals to sentiment and satisfies the imagination. We all wish it could be proved to be true. But it is misleading to teach it to American youth as history. It should be taught them as a legend — a tradition. Historically, the question of who made the first American Flag is still unanswered.

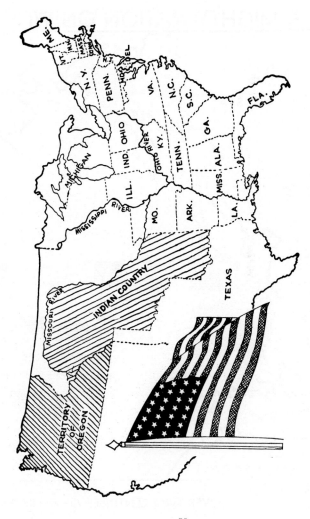

The American Flag in 1846

At the beginning of the Mexican War the Flag had twenty-eight stars.

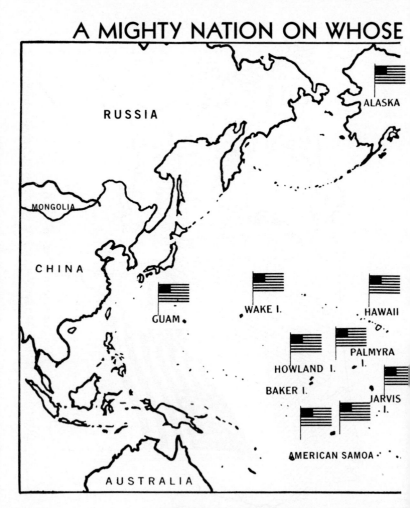

OVER TWO CENTURIES OF ACHIEVEMENT

FLAG THE SUN NEVER SETS

Shaded area represents territory that comprised the Thirteen Original States.

UNDER OUR AMERICAN SYSTEM OF GOVERNMENT

Raising the United States Flag in New Orleans, 1803

TERRITORIAL EXPANSION OF THE UNITED STATES

When the United States was born, July 4, 1776, it was but a strip along the Atlantic seaboard, with an area of about 850,000 square miles. As pioneers wended westward, more territory was acquired and more states were added to the Union; also, other territory came under the protection of the American Flag, until today the Stars and Stripes proudly waves over a great domain of almost 4,000,000 square miles. The following summary shows how the domain was acquired:

Continental United States (3,615,210 sq. miles). Acquired by the release of territory from Great Britain as a result of the War of the Revolution (*territory of the original thirteen states*); by purchase from France (*Louisiana Purchase, 1803*), Spain (*Florida Purchase, 1819*), Mexico (*Gadsden Purchase, 1853*); by accession from the Republic of Texas (admission of Texas as a state, 1845); by cession from Mexico after the Mexican War (more than half a million square miles in the southwest, 1848); and by discovery and exploration; *Alaska* (586,400 sq. miles) purchased from Russia in 1867, became a territory in 1912 and a state in 1959. Including the Aleutian Islands, it is more than twice the size of Texas.

Hawaii (6,423 sq. miles). Annexed in 1898 at the request of its citizens, the Hawaiian Islands were made a Territory of the United States on June 14, 1900, and became a state on August 21, 1959. The eight largest islands are: Hawaii, Kahoolawe, Kauai, Lanai, Maui, Molokai, Niihau and Oahu.

Puerto Rico (3,515 sq. miles). Ceded by Spain in 1898 by treaty of peace terminating the Spanish-American War.

Virgin Islands (former Danish West Indies — 133 sq. miles). Purchased from Denmark in 1917 for $25,000,000. They comprise the islands of St. Thomas, St. John, Saint Croix, and the adjacent islets.

Midway Island (2 sq. miles). An atoll and two islets discovered by an American in 1859, annexed in 1867, Midway is now an important air base.

Wake Island (3 sq. miles). Possession on behalf of the United States was taken January 17, 1899, by the commander of the U.S.S. "Bennington."

American Samoa (Tutuila Island, the largest of the Samoan Islands, and three other islands, with a total area of 77 sq. miles). Acquired in 1899 by arrangement with Great Britain and Germany.

Guam (209 sq. miles). Ceded by Spain in 1898 by treaty of peace terminating the Spanish-American War.

Trust Territory of the Pacific Islands. German possessions until 1922, then a Japanese mandate, these became a United Nations Trust Territory under the United States in 1947, headquartered at Pearl Harbor, Hawaii. The Territory now comprises **Palau (Belau)** (196 sq. miles). Originally the territory included the **Northern Mariana Islands** (184 sq. miles), now a Commonwealth, and the **Caroline Islands**, now a part of the Federated States of Micronesia (271 sq. miles) and **Marshall Islands** (70 sq. miles), now Republics in free association with the United States.

IMPORTANT FLAG ANNIVERSARIES

January 1. The Grand Union Flag, the first flag of the United Colonies, was displayed for the first time at Washington's headquarters, Cambridge, Massachusetts, January 1, 1776.

January 26. The United States frigate "Essex" was the first warship to fly the American Flag in the Pacific, January 26, 1813.

January 28. The first display of the American Flag in an attack against a foreign stronghold was at Nassau, Bahama Islands, when, on January 28, 1778, the Americans captured Fort Nassau from the British and raised the Stars and Stripes.

February 14. The first foreign salute to the Stars and Stripes was rendered February 14, 1778, when John Paul Jones, in command of the U.S.S. "Ranger," entered Quiberon Bay, near Brest, France, and received a salute of nine guns.

April 6. Admiral Robert E. Peary, on April 6, 1909, planted the American Flag at the North Pole.

June 14. The First Flag of the United States was adopted by Congress, June 14, 1777.

August 3. The first display of the Stars and Stripes by the Continental Army took place when the Flag was hoisted over Fort Stanwix, New York (the present site of Rome) during the attack by the British, August 3, 1777.

October 17. The American Flag was first saluted by the British at the surrender of Burgoyne's army, October 17, 1777.

October 18. The American Flag was first officially displayed over Alaska at Sitka, October 18, 1867.

THE STAR-SPANGLED BANNER*

O say, can you see by the dawn's early light
  What so proudly we hail'd at the twilight's last gleaming,
Whose broad stripes and bright stars, through the perilous
        fight,
    O'er the ramparts we watch'd, were so gallantly streaming?
      And the rocket's red glare, the bombs bursting in air,
        Gave proof through the night that our flag was still there.
      O say, does that star-spangled banner yet wave
      O'er the land of the free and the home of the brave?

On the shore dimly seen through the mists of the deep,
  Where the foe's haughty host in dread silence reposes,
What is that which the breeze, o'er the towering steep,
    As it fitfully blows, half conceals, half discloses?
      Now it catches the gleam of the morning's first beam
        In full glory reflected now shines on the stream.
      'Tis the star-spangled banner — O long may it wave
      O'er the land of the free and the home of the brave.

O thus be it e'er when freemen shall stand
  Between their lov'd home and the war's desolation!
Blest with vict'ry and peace may the heav'n rescued land
    Praise the Pow'r that hath made and preserved us a nation!
      Then conquer we must when our cause it is just,
        And this be our motto — "In God is our trust."
      And the star-spangled banner in triumph shall wave
      O'er the land of the free and the home of the brave.
                                    — FRANCIS SCOTT KEY, 1814

*The National Education Association in 1912 recommended the above
version as the authorized version of "The Star-Spangled Banner." In 1931
Congress enacted a law making the song our national anthem.

BIRTH OF OUR NATIONAL ANTHEM

No anthem ever written has a more historic, inspiring, and patriotic setting than "The Star-Spangled Banner," which was composed in 1814 when the United States and England were at war. After the British redcoats had burned Washington, the enemy moved on Baltimore, where the soldiers were to attack by land while a powerful British fleet formed for action off Fort McHenry, at the water gates of the city. All during the night of September 13–14, the entire fleet concentrated its fire on the Fort, from whose flagpole flew the Star-Spangled Banner.

Francis Scott Key, from the District of Columbia, was held as a captive on one of the British warships. As the battle raged throughout the night, in silence and darkness he paced the deck of the ship, wondering whether the Flag he had seen when the fight began was still flying over the Fort. It was for him a harrowing night.

At last came the break of day. With strained, eager eyes, through the early morning mist, he saw that the Flag was still there. In patriotic exultation Francis Scott Key, writing on an envelope he had found in his pocket, poured out of his soul the inspiring words of "The Star-Spangled Banner," which later were set to music. Thus the song went forth to sing itself into the hearts of the living generation and of generations to come.

———

A SONG FOR FLAG DAY*

Your flag and my flag,
    And how it flies to-day
In your land and my land
    And half a world away!
Rose-red and blood-red
    The stripes for ever gleam;
Snow-white and soul-white —
    The good forefathers' dream;

Sky-blue and true blue, with stars to gleam aright —
The gloried guidon of the day; a shelter through the night.

Your flag and my flag!
    And, oh, how much it holds —

*From *The Trail to Boyland*, by Wilbur D. Nesbit, copyright 1904, 1932. Used by special permission of the publishers, The Bobbs-Merrill Company.

Your land and my land—
    Secure within its folds!
Your heart and my heart
    Beat quicker at the sight;
Sun-kissed and wind-tossed—
    Red and blue and white.

The one flag—the great flag—the flag for me and you—
Glorified all else beside—the red and white and blue!

Your flag and my flag!
    To every star and stripe
The drums beat as hearts beat
    And fifers shrilly pipe!
Your flag and my flag—
    A blessing in the sky;
Your hope and my hope—
    It never hid a lie!

Home land and far land and half the world around,
Old Glory hears our glad salute and ripples to the sound!
                              —WILBUR D. NESBIT

————

THE FLAG GOES BY*

Hats off!
Along the street there comes
A blare of bugles, a ruffle of drums,
A flash of color beneath the sky:

*Used by permission of A. S. Barnes and Company.

> Hats off!
> The Flag is passing by!
> Blue and crimson and white it shines,
> Over the steel-tipped, ordered lines.
> Hats off!
> The colors before us fly;
> But more than the flag is passing by.

> Sea-fights and land-fights, grim and great,
> Fought to make and to save the State:
> Weary marches and sinking ships;
> Cheers of victory on dying lips;

> Days of plenty and years of peace;
> March of a strong land's swift increase;
> Equal justice, right, and law,
> Stately honor and reverend awe;

> Sign of a nation, great and strong
> To ward her people from foreign wrong:
> Pride and glory and honor — all
> Live in the colors to stand or fall.

> Hats off!
> Along the street there comes
> A blare of bugles, a ruffle of drums,
> And loyal hearts are beating high:
> Hats off!
> The flag is passing by!

— HENRY HOLCOMB BENNETT

THE STORY OF "OLD GLORY"

Nearly two centuries ago — on March 17, 1824 — in Salem, Massachusetts, upon the occasion of the celebration of his twenty-first birthday, William Driver was presented by his mother and a group of Salem girls with a beautiful American Flag.

"I name her 'Old Glory,'" said he, in response to the greetings of the givers, and thus it was that the name "Old Glory" made its advent into the history of our Flag. William Driver's heart and soul were in his occupation of sailing the seas, and from that day on, "Old Glory" accompanied William Driver whenever he went to sea. When, in 1837, after many notable voyages Captain Driver quit the sea and settled in Nashville, Tennessee, "Old Glory" as usual accompanied him. On historic occasions it could be seen gracefully waving from a rope extending from the Captain's house to a tree across the street.

One day, not long before his death, the old Captain placed in the arms of his daughter a bundle, saying:

"Mary Jane, this is my old ship flag, 'Old Glory.' It has been my constant companion on many voyages. I love it as a mother loves her child; take it and cherish it as I have cherished it, for it has been my steadfast friend and protector in all parts of the world, among savages, heathen, and civilized. Keep it always."

"Old Glory" was kept and guarded as a precious heirloom in the Driver family until 1922, when it was sent to the Smithsonian Institution in Washington where it is today, carefully preserved under glass. Every year it is seen by thousands of loyal Americans who visit the capital of their country.

FLAG DAY

June 14, the anniversary of the adoption of the Flag of the United States in 1777, is now quite generally observed as Flag Day.

There are many persons who, in all sincerity, claim the credit of having originated Flag Day. Some of these claimants did do commendable and serious initiative work *locally,* and were honest in their belief that they had originated Flag Day, but they were in ignorance of the fact that patriotic individuals and organizations in other parts of the United States had started similar work years earlier.

June 14 was definitely established as Flag Day by a Proclamation of President Wilson, issued May 30, 1916, in which he said, in part:

"It has, therefore, seemed to me fitting that I should call your attention to the approach of the anniversary of the day upon which the Flag of the United States was adopted by the Congress as the emblem of the Union, and to suggest to you that it should this year and in the years to come be given special significance....

"I therefore suggest and request that throughout the nation, and, if possible, in every community, the fourteenth day of June be observed as FLAG DAY, with special patriotic exercises, at which means shall be taken to give significant expression to our thoughtful love of America...our determination to make it greater and purer...."

The above Proclamation of President Wilson was the culmination of a quarter of a century of separate and unconnected efforts by individuals and organizations in different parts of the country in the interest of the observance of June 14 as Flag Day.

HOW TO DISPLAY THE FLAG

In June of 1923 and 1924, National Flag Conferences attended by representatives from the Army, the Navy, and the principal patriotic, civic, and educational organizations of the country, were held in Washington for the purpose of formulating and adopting a Flag Code prescribing correct ways of displaying and respecting the Flag of the United States. In addressing the opening sessions of the 1923 Conference, President Harding said:

"Everything we do to bring the Flag into proper consideration by the citizenship of the Republic is highly commendable and deserves to be cordially indorsed."

The rules for Flag display that follow are based on the Code that was adopted by the National Flag Conferences and later enacted into law by Congress in 1942 (Public Law 829), and amended in 1976 (Public Law 94-344).

GENERAL RULES

It is the universal custom to display the flag only from sunrise to sunset on buildings and on stationary flagstaffs in the open. However, when a patriotic effect is desired, the flag may be displayed twenty-four hours a day if properly illuminated during the hours of darkness.

The Flag should not be flown in rainy or stormy weather, except when an all-weather flag is displayed.

The Flag should always be raised briskly and lowered slowly and ceremoniously.

When the Flag is being raised or lowered, it must never be allowed to touch the ground.

In a procession with another flag:

The United States Flag is on the marching right.

In a procession with a line of other flags:

The bearer of the Flag marches alone in the center of the line.

When displayed either vertically or horizontally against a wall, in a show window, or elsewhere:

The blue field is uppermost and to the Flag's own right—that is, to the observer's left.

When used on a speaker's platform:

(a) If displayed flat, the Flag is above and behind the speaker.
(b) If flown from a staff, the Flag is in the position of honor, at the speaker's right, and preferably slightly in front.

When displayed from a staff projecting horizontally or at an angle from the window sill, balcony, or front of a building:

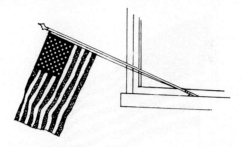

The blue field of the Flag goes clear to the peak.

When displayed with another flag against a wall, staffs crossed:

The United States Flag is on the observer's left, and its staff is in front of the staff of the other flag.

When flown on the same halyard with flags of states or cities, or pennants of societies:

The United States Flag is at the peak.

NOTES

1. In the Navy the church pennant — which, by the way, is not the flag of the church but a signal flag to indicate that services are being conducted — is flown above the National Flag according to Navy custom while naval chaplains conduct services at sea.

2. It is considered better form never to fly any other flag on the same staff with the Flag of the United States, but instead to fly the other flag on another staff.

When the United States Flag and flags of other nations, states, or cities, or pennants of societies, are flown from adjacent staffs:

*The United States Flag is on the right of the line—
that is, on the observer's left.*

NOTES

1. When the United States Flag and flags of other nations, states, or cities, or pennants of societies, are flown from adjacent staffs, the United States Flag is hoisted first and lowered last.

2. When the United States Flag is flown with flags of other nations, all staffs should be of the same height and the flags of approximately equal size. An exception to this rule is that the flag of the United Nations flies above all other flags at UN headquarters in New York City.

3. International usage forbids the display of the flag of any one nation above that of any other nation in time of peace.

In a group of flags of states or cities, or pennants of societies, displayed from staffs:

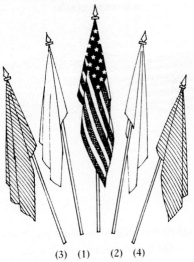

(3) (1)   (2) (4)

The United States Flag is at the center and at the highest point of the group.

NOTE

In a group of flags of different nations, an arrangement to which no one could take exception would be to place the flags alphabetically, alternately on the right and on the left of the United States Flag. For example, in the case of France, Germany, Great Britain, and Japan, the flag of France would occupy the position (1), Germany (2), Great Britain (3), and Japan (4). At headquarters of international organizations, such as the UN, flags are flown in the alphabetical order of their country names in English.

When suspended over a sidewalk from a rope, extending from a house to a pole at the edge of the sidewalk:

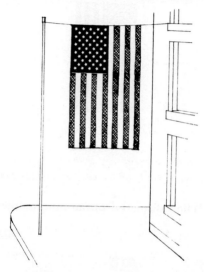

The Flag is hoisted a part of the way out from the building, toward the pole, blue field first.

On a float in a parade:

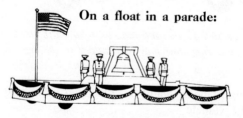

The Flag is displayed from a staff with folds falling free, or hung flat.

When displayed over the middle of a street:

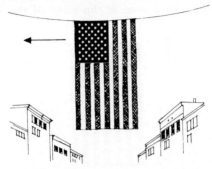

The Flag is suspended vertically, with the blue field to the north in an east-and-west street, or the east in a north-and-south street.

When displayed on an automobile:

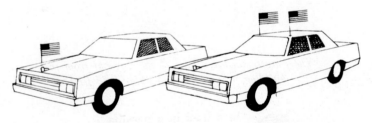

The Flag may be tied to the antenna, or to a staff fixed firmly to the chassis, or a flag staff may be clamped to the right fender.

NOTE

Under no circumstances should the Flag ever be draped over any part of the vehicle.

When displayed in a church or synagogue:

The United States Flag is in the position of honor at the clergy's right facing the congregation, and the church or other flag is at the left.

NOTE

This rule for the display of the Flag applies to any other building or auditorium.

To indicate mourning when the Flag is flown from a stationary staff:

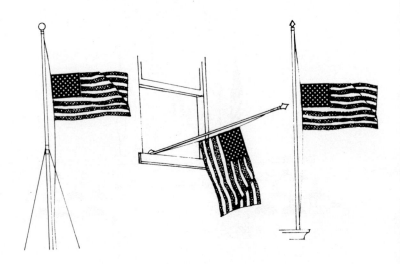

The Flag is placed at half-staff.

NOTES

1. The position of half-staff, or half-mast, is considered to be some distance (not necessarily halfway down) from the top of the staff.

2. When the Flag is to be flown at half-staff, it should be hoisted to the peak for an instant and then lowered to the half-staff. Before being lowered for the day, the Flag should be raised to the peak.

When used to cover a casket:

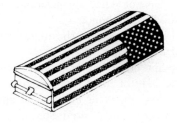

The union of the Flag is at the head of the casket and over the left shoulder of the deceased.

NOTES

1. The casket should be carried foot first.

2. The Flag must not be lowered into the grave, or allowed to touch the ground.

CAUTIONS TO OBSERVE IN DISPLAY

1. Do not permit disrespect to be shown to the Flag.
2. Do not dip the Flag to any person or any thing. The regimental color or state, organization, or institutional flag will render this honor.
3. Do not display the Flag with the union down except as a signal of distress.
4. Do not place any other flag or pennant above or to the right of the Flag of the United States.
5. Do not place any object or emblem of any kind on or above the Flag of the United States.
6. Do not use the Flag as drapery in any form whatsoever. Use bunting of red, white, and blue.
7. Do not drape the Flag over the hood, top, sides, or back of a vehicle, or of a railway train or boat.
8. Do not use the Flag as a covering for a ceiling.
9. Do not carry the Flag flat or horizontally, but always aloft and free.
10. Do not let the Flag touch the ground or the floor, or trail in the water.
11. No part of the Flag should ever be used as a costume or athletic uniform. However, a Flag patch may be affixed to the uniform of military personnel, firefighters, police and members of patriotic organizations. Do not embroider it upon cushions or handkerchiefs or print it on paper napkins or boxes.
12. Do not put lettering of any kind upon the Flag.
13. Do not use the Flag in any form of advertising or fasten an advertising sign to a pole from which the Flag is flown.
14. Do not display, use, or store the Flag in such a manner as will permit it to be easily soiled or damaged.

FLAG NEVER TO BE DRAPED

The Flag of the United States is an artistic, well-proportioned emblem whose beauty should not be marred by draping. Draping may be done with red, white, and blue bunting, but not with the Flag.

Bunting of the national colors should be used over the front of a platform and for decoration in general. The bunting must always be arranged with the blue on top, or to the observer's left, white in the middle, and red below or to the observer's right. *The reason for this is that the blue, being the color of the union of the Flag, is the "honor color," and should therefore come first, either horizontally or vertically.*

DESTRUCTION OF UNSIGHTLY FLAGS

Torn, soiled, or badly faded Flags should not be displayed. Flags may be mended, dry-cleaned or washed. When a Flag is in such a condition that it is no longer a fitting emblem to display, it should be destroyed as a whole, privately, preferably by burning or by some other method lacking in any suggestion of irreverence or disrespect.

WHEN TO DISPLAY THE FLAG

A citizen may fly the Flag on any day. The Flag should be displayed on all National and State Holidays, on historic and special occasions, and other such days as may be proclaimed by the President.

PRINCIPAL LEGAL AND PUBLIC HOLIDAYS

Most legal holidays falling on a Sunday or Saturday are observed the Friday before, or the Monday following the date.

January 1. New Year's Day.

January 15, or Third Monday in January. Martin Luther King Day.

January 20, every fourth year. Presidential Inauguration Day.

February 12. Lincoln's Birthday.

Third Monday in February. Washington's Birthday (Presidents' Day, Washington-Lincoln Day).

Last Monday in May. Memorial Day (Decoration Day). Flag to be at half-staff until noon, full staff from noon to sunset.

June 14. Flag Day.

July 4. Independence Day.

First Monday in September. Labor Day.

Second Monday in October. Columbus Day (Discovery Day, Pioneers' Day).

First Tuesday after the first Monday in November. Election Day.

November 11. Veterans' Day.

Fourth Thursday in November. Thanksgiving Day.

December 25. Christmas Day.

In the various states the Flag should be displayed on **Admission Day, State Holidays,** and all **Election Days.**

SALUTING THE FLAG

During the ceremony of hoisting or lowering the Flag, or when the Flag is passing in a parade, everyone present should face the Flag, stand at attention, and salute.

Those in uniform should render the military salute. When

not in uniform, a man should remove his hat with the right hand and hold it at the left shoulder, the hand being over the heart.

Women, and men without hats, should salute the Flag by placing the right hand over the heart. Women do not remove their hats when saluting the Flag.

The Flag is saluted the moment it passes by in a parade or review.

SALUTE TO THE NATIONAL ANTHEM

When "The Star-Spangled Banner" is played, everyone present should stand at attention and salute as described above. The salute is rendered at the first note of the anthem, and the position is retained until the last note.

PLEDGE TO THE FLAG

In pledging allegiance to the Flag of the United States, the approved practice in schools, which is suitable for civilian adults, is as follows:

Standing, with the right hand over the heart, all the pupils repeat together:

I pledge allegiance to the Flag of the United States of America, and to the Republic for which it stands, one nation, under God, indivisible, with liberty and justice for all.

However, civilian adults will always show full respect to the Flag, when the pledge is being given, by merely standing at attention, men removing their hats.

Persons in uniform should render the military salute.

COAT OF ARMS
OF THE UNITED STATES

The Coat of Arms of the United States consists of an eagle with wings and feet outspread and bearing the following distinguishing devices:

Shield. On the eagle's breast is the *Shield of the United States*, consisting of thirteen vertical stripes, symbolizing the thirteen original states. The blue upper part of the shield is called the *chief*.

Crest. The crest over the head of the eagle shows thirteen stars breaking through a cloud, denoting a new constellation in the firmament of sovereign powers.

E pluribus unum. This Latin phrase, "One out of Many," alludes to the one Union formed out of many states.

Olive branch and arrows. The olive branch and the arrows (thirteen) in the talons of the eagle denote the power of peace and war which is vested in Congress.

The Coat of Arms of the United States should be used only by those who are authorized by law and custom to do so. Under no circumstances should the Coat of Arms or the Shield of the United States be used for advertising purposes.

FLAG LAWS

Both the federal government and the states have passed laws relating to the display and use of the Flag.

FEDERAL FLAG LAWS

In addition to the law of June 14, 1777, adopting the Flag, and subsequent laws affecting the design of the Flag, Congress has so far passed six laws regarding the Flag:

1. *Trademarks.* The Act of Congress of February 20, 1905, provides that a trademark cannot be registered which consists of, or comprises among other things, "the Flag, coat of arms, or other insignia of the United States, or any simulation thereof."

2. *Mother's Day.* A joint resolution of Congress, approved May 8, 1914, enjoins the display of the Flag on Mother's Day.

3. *Prevention of desecration in District of Columbia.* The Act of February 8, 1917, provides certain penalties for the desecration, mutilation, or improper use of the Flag within the District of Columbia.

4. *Dismissal from government service.* The Act of May 16, 1918, provides for the dismissal from the service, when the United States is at war, of any employee or official of the United States government who criticizes in an abusive or violent manner the Flag of the United States.

5. *Flag Code.* A joint resolution of Congress, approved June 22, 1942, codifies the existing rules and customs pertaining to the display and use of the Flag.

6. *Flag Code, amended.* A joint resolution of Congress, approved December 22, 1942, amends the Flag Code resolution approved June 22, 1942. The code was again amended July 7, 1976.

STATE FLAG LAWS

Every state in the Union has a law prohibiting the abuse, misuse, or desecration of the Flag of the United States. In most cases the provisions of the law cover also the abuse, misuse, or desecration of the state flag; also, in many cases, the misuse or desecration of the national and of the state shields and coats of arms.

The purpose of these laws is to prevent and punish: *(a)* the placing of any word, figure, mark, picture, design, drawing, or advertisement of whatever nature upon the Flag of the United States, or upon any picture or other representation of the Flag of the United States; and *(b)* the mutilation, defacement, defiance, abuse, or improper use of the Flag, including the use of the Flag for the purpose of advertising the sale of merchandise.

FLAG OF UNITED STATES DEFINED

According to the Flag laws of the District of Columbia and nearly all the states, the words "Flag of the United States" include any flag, or any picture of any flag, in which the colors, the stars, and the stripes may be shown in any number which, without careful examination or deliberation, the average person may believe to represent the Flag of the United States.

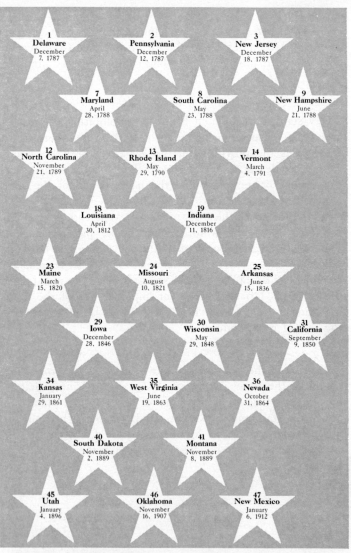

EVERY STAR A STATE — EVERY STATE A STAR

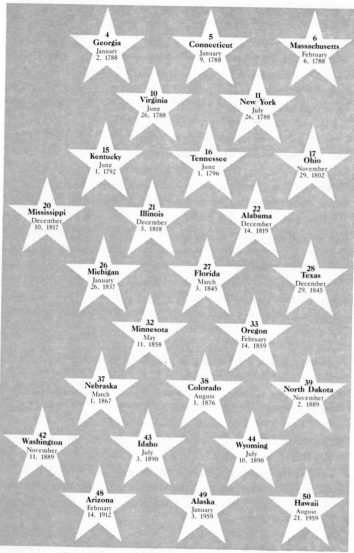

Pick out the star of your state

GLOSSARY OF FLAG TERMS

canton: a rectangular division of a flag or ensign, usually in the upper corner next to the staff and containing the national or other device

color: in the military service, the national flag carried by unmounted units. The expression, "The Colors," is used quite generally in referring to a flag

dip: to lower a flag as a salute

ensign: in the Navy, the term for the national flag

field: the ground of each division in a flag

fly: the side of a flag extending from the staff to the flying end — that is, the long side

half-mast: to lower a flag some distance (not necessarily halfway down) from the top of the staff, as a token of mourning

halyard: a rope or cord with which a flag is drawn to the top of the staff, and with which it is lowered

hoist: the side of a flag extending along the staff — that is, the short side. To *hoist* a flag is to raise it to the top of the staff

increscent: the new moon depicted with the points turned toward the dexter (right) side

standard: the national flag carried in the military service by mounted or motorized units

strike: to haul a flag down in token of surrender

union: a design emblematic of union, used on a national flag or ensign, sometimes covering the whole field, sometimes occupying an upper inner corner. The union of the Flag of the United States is the cluster of fifty stars on the field of blue, symbolizing the union of the states.

THE INDEX

PART III

Presidents

OF OUR UNITED STATES

By L. A. Esler

GEORGE WASHINGTON

1st President

Born February 22, 1732   Died December 14, 1799

President 1789–1797

"First in war, first in peace, and first in the hearts of his countrymen." These words, first written of Washington at the time of his death, describe the immortal place that he holds in history and in the affections of the American people.

Born in Westmoreland County, Virginia, Washington preferred a life of service to his country, with all its responsibilities and hardships, to the life of comfort which his wealth and his station as the son of a prosperous planter assured him.

As a young man he established a reputation for truthfulness, honesty, and forthrightness. He worked hard and performed his tasks with great care and accuracy.

In his first military engagements and with General Braddock, Washington showed courage and sound judgment. In civil life he attended many public assemblies, served in the Virginia House of Burgesses, and, while a member of the Second Continental Congress, was chosen commander in chief of the Continental Army.

After his brilliant achievements in the American Revolution, Washington exerted his immense influence in behalf of a stronger central government. Six years after his resignation as commander in chief he was unanimously chosen the first President of the United States.

Admission of three new states, Vermont, Kentucky, and Tennessee, to the Union; establishment of the First Bank of the United States; and the adoption of the first ten amendments to the Constitution were important events of Washington's term. Also, for the first time, the popular vote fell into two definite groups or political parties—the Federalists and the Republicans. It was indeed fortunate for the nation that these early years of the new government were under the able leadership of George Washington.

Photo from Paul's Photos

JOHN ADAMS

2d President

Born October 19, 1735   Died July 4, 1826

President 1797-1801

Braintree, Massachusetts, was the birthplace of John Adams, son of a respected, well-to-do farmer.

Adams wanted to become a clergyman when he was graduated from Harvard, but he decided to teach and to study law. He liked to write, and he took an active interest in public affairs.

Adams' marriage to the daughter of a prominent Massachusetts clergyman widened his acquaintance and extended his influence. He frequently held public office. His varied duties gave him wide experience and numerous responsibilities. As commissioner to France, and later as the first United States minister to England, his influence was felt beyond American boundaries. He often worked with Thomas Jefferson in public matters; they both signed the Declaration of Independence. While Adams was vice president under Washington, Jefferson was a member of Washington's cabinet.

Adams was a Federalist; Jefferson, a leader of the Democratic-Republican party. Both were candidates for President at the close of Washington's second term. Adams won the election by only three votes, and Jefferson was made vice president. Difference of political views and sympathies drew them apart, although they continued to have sincere respect for each other.

One of Adams' last important acts as President was to make a peaceable settlement of difficulties with France. The naval war with France had seemed to unite the two political parties, but controversies soon began and party strife became acute. Alexander Hamilton, a Federalist but an enemy of Adams, made bitter attacks upon Adams' policies. In this political turmoil Adams was defeated for a second term. In spite of the many unhappy memories of his own term as President, he is the only President who has ever had the joy of seeing his son elected to that position.

THOMAS JEFFERSON

3d President

Born April 13, 1743   Died July 4, 1826

President 1801-1809

Thomas Jefferson was the second Virginian to be elected President. He was born at Shadwell, Albemarle County. When Jefferson was only fourteen, his father died and left him with the care of a large family, but he also left him some land and an honored name in the community.

Jefferson inherited his father's aptness for mathematics, his love for exploring new country, and his ability to draw. Attending William and Mary College, he acquired both classical and practical knowledge. Law, however, was his chosen profession and a means by which he greatly increased his own fortune.

After his marriage he built his home, "Monticello," at the top of one of his native hills. His skill as a horseman and his musical talents added much to his social charm and popularity. Because of his literary ability, he was often asked to write papers of various kinds, and the honor of writing the Declaration of Independence was his.

A leader of democratic ideals and an able public servant, Jefferson was elected by the Republican party to succeed John Adams, a Federalist, as President. Jefferson was a popular man and a popular President. One of his most important presidential acts, in its effect upon the country, was his purchase from the French of the Louisiana Territory, which at that time doubled the size of the United States.

It was a coincidence of fate that Thomas Jefferson and John Adams, the only two Presidents who signed the Declaration of Independence, should die on the same day, and that the day should be the anniversary of their act—July fourth.

Photo from Brown Brothers

JAMES MADISON

4th President

Born March 16, 1751   Died June 28, 1836

President 1809-1817

James Madison, born at Port Conway, Virginia, was the son of a planter.

It was Madison's good fortune to receive excellent instruction when he was young. Later his fondness for study easily carried him through his courses at Princeton. There he became interested in many subjects, including law, theology, philosophy, languages, and civil government.

Madison was an admirer and a friend of Jefferson, and he served as secretary of state during Jefferson's term of office as President.

With a trained mind, but small of stature and none too rugged, Madison was more fitted for a statesman than a soldier. He earned the title, "Father of the Constitution," because of the large share he had in drafting the original articles, and because he wrote the first ten amendments that were ratified and adopted.

Madison, a Democratic-Republican, was elected President to succeed Jefferson. Always a peace-loving man, Madison was reluctant to consent to another war with England. Finally he decided it was necessary, and the War of 1812 was fought against England to establish the commercial rights of the United States on the sea. The Treaty of Ghent in 1814 brought the war to a close.

Completing two terms in the White House, President and Mrs. Madison retired to the peace and quiet of Madison's boyhood home at Montpelier, Virginia, where Madison took an active interest in public affairs and spent his time writing, until his death.

JAMES MONROE

5th President

Born April 28, 1758   Died July 4, 1831

President 1817-1825

James Monroe was born in Westmoreland County, Virginia, the son of parents of modest means.

Monroe received a good education, but he left William and Mary College to enlist in the Revolutionary War. His size, strength, and endurance fitted him for such hardships as he met in the colonial army. After the war, like many of his associates, he turned to law and politics for his life work. He held a succession of posts in the Virginia legislature, Continental Congress, Virginia Ratifying Convention, the United States Senate, and the diplomatic service in France and England. He also served as governor of Virginia, and as secretary of state and secretary of war under Madison. He was thoroughly familiar with his country's business and well fitted for the duties of President, to which office he was elected by the Democratic-Republican party.

The thing by which Monroe is best known to the American people is his declaration of the independent position of the United States with regard to further colonization in America by European countries, and of non-interference of the United States in the domestic affairs of Europe. This policy is known as the Monroe Doctrine.

Other important accomplishments of Monroe's eight years as President are the pledge of peace made between England and the United States in 1817 over the Canadian frontier line, the annexation of Florida by purchase from Spain in 1819, and the Missouri Compromise of 1820.

After a life spent in service to his country, James Monroe died at the age of seventy-three in New York City.

JOHN QUINCY ADAMS

6th President

Born July 11, 1767   Died February 23, 1848

President 1825–1829

John Quincy Adams was born at his father's birthplace, Braintree, Massachusetts. As a child John Quincy traveled with his father, who was sent to European countries on various diplomatic missions. He was often in the presence of statesmen, soldiers, and politicians. At fourteen he was secretary to the United States minister to Russia.

Adams completed his studies at Harvard and established himself in the practice of law. Again he crossed the Atlantic, this time as minister to Holland, and on this trip he married the daughter of an American diplomat in London. He represented the United States as minister to Prussia, minister to England, and minister to Russia. In 1802 he was a member of the Massachusetts Senate and the next year, of the United States Senate. During the War of 1812, President Madison sent Adams to England to negotiate the terms of peace which finally resulted in the Treaty of Ghent.

With proud independence John Quincy Adams defended, often alone, the things he thought to be right. His political ideas helped to shape the policies of the National-Republican party which represented a coalition between his supporters and those of Henry Clay. The Democratic-Republican party of Jefferson's time became the Democratic party. Those issues which so sharply divided Federalists and Jeffersonians when John Adams was President were less pronounced during the presidency of his son, John Quincy Adams.

The four years of John Quincy Adams' administration were chiefly devoted to improving the efficiency of all branches of the government and to extending United States commerce with foreign countries.

After Adams left the presidency he returned to Washington as a representative in Congress—a step which no other President has taken. At the age of eighty-one, while he was attending the regular session of Congress, he was fatally stricken.

ANDREW JACKSON

7th President

Born March 15, 1767   Died June 8, 1845

President 1829-1837

Andrew Jackson's parents were Scotch-Irish immigrants who settled in the wilderness along the border between North Carolina and South Carolina. There, at the Waxhaw settlement, Jackson was born.

He received most of his education in the school of experience. Strong and enthusiastic, Jackson enjoyed many rough sports. He was a fearless youth and always true to his friends.

As a young man Jackson became interested in and studied law. He moved to Tennessee and built a comfortable home which he called "The Hermitage." He was a delegate to the state convention, helped frame the state constitution, and was elected to the one seat in the national House of Representatives to which Tennessee was entitled. In spite of his continued association with statesmen, Jackson never lost his brusque manners and impulsive disposition.

Jackson and his sharpshooters fought the final, victorious Battle of New Orleans in the War of 1812. Peace with England had already been made, but neither side knew it, and Jackson was hailed as a hero. Invading Florida in the Seminole War, he was again victorious, and later became governor of that territory.

The common people liked Jackson. Political leaders saw in this devotion a chance for building a strong Democratic party by making Jackson a candidate for President. With wild enthusiasm he was elected. As President, Jackson opposed the Bank of the United States. He withdrew all public funds there deposited, and refused to renew the charter. By placing his political favorites in office he encouraged the "spoils system."

Jackson, a powerful and popular figure, holds a unique place in the political history of the nation.

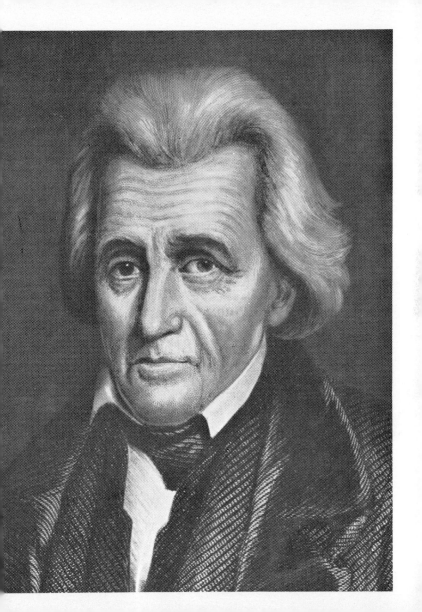

MARTIN VAN BUREN

8th President

Born December 5, 1782

Died July 24, 1862

President 1837-1841

Of Dutch descent, Martin Van Buren was born at Kinderhook, New York.

Getting what schooling he could, Van Buren began the study of law when he was fourteen and eventually rose to the top of his profession. He was interested in politics, became a clever political leader, and was one of the group who controlled New York politics. Van Buren was appointed attorney general of New York, then elected to the United States Senate, and later was made governor of New York.

Because he was an ardent Democrat, Martin Van Buren did as much as he could to aid his friend, Andrew Jackson, and was largely responsible for the first Democratic National Convention. As secretary of state in Jackson's cabinet he had a large share in shaping national policies. He served as vice president during Jackson's second term and was elected President in 1836.

The panic of 1837 emphasized the question of the method of handling public money, and it was on that issue that Van Buren is said to have made his greatest contribution as a statesman. He established an independent treasury system which, with changes and improvements, is still in use.

Throughout Van Buren's single term of office, war with the Seminole Indians, revolutionary disturbances both in Mexico and Ontario, and a financial panic with labor disturbances involved, created political discontent and made it impossible for Van Buren to be re-elected. He was active in politics for many years after he left the White House. He died, when almost eighty, in his native town of Kinderhook, New York.

WILLIAM HENRY HARRISON

9th President

Born February 9, 1773   Died April 4, 1841

President 1841-April 4, 1841

William Henry Harrison, born at Berkeley, Charles County, Virginia, was the son of one of Virginia's colonial statesmen.

Harrison's father, a signer of the Declaration of Independence, wanted his son to study medicine, and Harrison left Hampden-Sidney College with that purpose in mind. However, he wanted to be a soldier, and after his father's death he decided to enter military service.

As aid-de-camp, Harrison accompanied General Anthony Wayne in his military campaigns against the Indians throughout the Northwest Territory, where the white settlers were continually threatened by savage Indian tribes. For his work on this western frontier Harrison was made governor of this vast territory which extended from the Ohio River to the Rocky Mountains. He often had to outwit Indian treachery, as in the case of the Battle of Tippecanoe. In upper Canada Harrison helped win the Battle of the Thames against the combined Indian and British forces.

After serving in both houses of Congress and in the Ohio Senate, Harrison was appointed United States minister to Colombia. The position called for greater diplomacy than President Jackson thought Harrison showed, and Harrison was recalled. He then retired to his farm in Hamilton County, Ohio, where he became county recorder. His home was a center for small groups of Whig politicians. Harrison had few political enemies. He was chosen by the Whig party to head the presidential ticket, with John Tyler, of Virginia, for vice president. The popular slogan of the campaign was "Tippecanoe and Tyler too."

Only a month after he was inaugurated, he died of pneumonia in Washington, D. C.

JOHN TYLER

10th President

Born March 29, 1790   Died January 18, 1862

President April 4, 1841-1845

That John Tyler should become President was a surprise to the Whig party. It was Harrison's untimely death that made him President.

Tyler was born at Greenway, Charles City County, Virginia. He received a good education and chose the profession of law. He held public office in the Virginia House of Delegates, in both houses of Congress, and was governor of Virginia for one term.

Tyler had rigid views on matters of public policy, and little regard for party loyalty. Although he was a Democrat during most of Jackson's presidency, he disliked Jackson's despotic methods. Many southerners shared Tyler's views. Furthermore, his belief in states rights was agreeable to the "states-rights" Whigs. For that reason the Whig party thought Tyler would be a wise choice as a candidate for vice president—a post considered of little importance. The Whigs did not reckon with the trick of fate which was to make him President just a month after the inauguration.

Strict construction of the Constitution was one of Tyler's principles. Twice he vetoed a bill, presented by Whig leaders, to re-establish the Bank of the United States. His determined opposition angered the Whigs, and the entire cabinet, except Daniel Webster, resigned. From that time to the end of his term, "Honest John Tyler" had little sympathy and almost no co-operation from Congress, politicians, or voters.

Neither Whigs nor Democrats would support Tyler for re-election. He was never again a prominent political figure, but he later supported the Confederacy. He died at Richmond, Virginia.

JAMES KNOX POLK

11th President

Born November 2, 1795   Died June 15, 1849

President 1845-1849

James Knox Polk was born in Mecklenburg County, North
Carolina. His parents moved from there to Tennessee. Polk
received his education there and in North Carolina, where he
attended college. He began his practice of law in Tennessee
and was elected to the Tennessee legislature. For fourteen
years Tennessee sent him as a representative to the national
Congress, and then made him governor of the state.

Polk was not thought of as a possible candidate for President
at the beginning of the campaign of 1844. He was considered
for the vice presidency. Van Buren was the likeliest man to
receive the Democratic nomination, until he came out against
the annexation of Texas. Polk favored annexation, won the
nomination when the convention deadlocked, and defeated
Clay in the election.

As a national policy Polk opposed the establishment of a
national bank. He favored the independent treasury system
for handling public money. On the question of slavery he
sympathized with the South and actively opposed the anti-
slavery movement. But these questions, important as they
were, were overshadowed by the question of expansion.

Boundary rights, bitterly disputed by the United States
and Mexico, brought on the War with Mexico. With the
close of the war, the United States successfully completed the
annexation of 522,000 square miles of territory, for which
the sum of fifteen million dollars was paid to the Mexican
government.

Polk's sincerity, his kindness, and his courteous manners
were admitted even by men who disliked and opposed him.
He died only a few months after leaving the White House,
at his home in Nashville, Tennessee.

ZACHARY TAYLOR

12th President

Born November 24, 1784   Died July 9, 1850

President 1849-July 9, 1850

Zachary Taylor was born in Orange County, Virginia. Soon after his birth his parents went west to the Kentucky frontier, and Zachary spent his boyhood in the country around Louisville. He received scant education from the few, poorly equipped schools in the neighborhood. He wanted to be a soldier, and when he became a young man he enlisted in the regular army.

Taylor served with distinction in the War of 1812. He also led troops in the Indian wars with the Black Hawks and the Seminoles. After being stationed at various frontier posts on the Mexican border, he occupied the disputed ground on which war with Mexico began. His men gave him the friendly title, "Old Rough and Ready."

Never active in the affairs of civil government, Taylor was known only by his military successes. He won notable victories in the War with Mexico, which made him a popular hero. The Whigs saw in him, as a presidential candidate, a chance to capture the votes of southern Democrats, for Taylor was a southerner. He had been too busy fighting to take an active interest in political issues; consequently he had no political enemies. He seemed to be an acceptable candidate for President and was elected.

Taylor apparently reconciled the disagreements between North and South. California's request to come into the Union as a free rather than a slave state was a point of hot dispute. Taylor was willing to grant the request. Gold had just been discovered in California, and people were rushing westward. At Washington, Henry Clay was offering a solution of the great issues of the day in the notable Compromise of 1850.

As these important questions were being discussed, President Taylor died, just a little more than a year after his inauguration.

Photo from Brown Brothers

MILLARD FILLMORE

13th President

Born January 7, 1800   Died March 8, 1874

President July 9, 1850-1853

Millard Fillmore was born on a farm in Cayuga County, New York. There was little opportunity for him to go to school, and his parents apprenticed him to a clothier.

But young Fillmore rebelled against the cruel treatment he received during his apprenticeship, and before he completed his term he left to study law in East Aurora, New York. Finally he was admitted to practice and became partner in a well-known Buffalo law firm.

The prominence of his firm and his own success as a lawyer gave him a wide acquaintance throughout New York State. He was sent to the state legislature, later to Congress, and in the presidential campaign of 1848 was elected vice president.

When President Taylor died, Fillmore succeeded him to the presidency. He took office at the time when Daniel Webster, Henry Clay, John C. Calhoun, and others—the most gifted group of orators ever assembled at one time in the United States Senate—were having heated debates on the most vital issues of the day, summed up in the Compromise of 1850. Although President Taylor had opposed this measure, President Fillmore approved it. Feeling ran high on both sides, and the slavery question so divided Whigs and Democrats that party lines between them were no longer clearly drawn.

The presidential campaign of 1852 was waged in a state of general confusion. President Fillmore failed to receive the nomination of his party, and the Whig party soon passed into history.

Although he traveled, was interested in public questions, and took active part in civic affairs, Fillmore never again held high political office. He spent the remainder of his life enjoying the comforts of his spacious home in Buffalo.

Photo from Brown Brothers

FRANKLIN PIERCE

14th President

Born November 23, 1804   Died October 8, 1869

President 1853-1857

Franklin Pierce was born in the town of Hillsboro, New Hampshire, and after completing his studies at Bowdoin College was admitted to practice law.

Young Pierce had an enthusiastic love for his country. He took an interest in public affairs and entered politics as soon as he finished his study of law. His election to the state legislature and to both houses of Congress followed. He was a Democrat and an ardent admirer of Andrew Jackson.

In the War with Mexico, Pierce enlisted as a private, and the following year was commissioned a brigadier general. He was not forceful as a soldier or politician, but people liked him. He made few enemies, and so was acceptable to political leaders as a presidential candidate at a time when other candidates were engaging in bitter rivalry. He carried all except four of the states in the Union.

During his presidency the United States purchased from Mexico forty-five thousand square miles of land along the southwestern border, Japanese ports were opened to American commerce, and plans were laid for the first railroad across the continent to the Pacific. With the passing of the Kansas-Nebraska Bill, which Pierce approved, the question of slavery was again at white heat. Politicians believed that the situation demanded greater statesmanship than Pierce had shown, and he was not renominated.

At the end of his term he retired from the presidency and from public life to travel and to spend the remainder of his life in his New England home.

JAMES BUCHANAN

15th President

Born April 23, 1791   Died June 1, 1868

President 1857-1861

James Buchanan was born near Mercersburg, Pennsylvania. His Scotch-Irish parents were thrifty and prosperous.

After receiving a good general education, followed by three years' study of law, Buchanan was admitted to practice. He was successful from the first and showed such talent for making speeches and debating that he attracted the attention of politicians. Although he enlisted in the War of 1812, he saw no real action. During the war he was elected to the Pennsylvania legislature. This was the beginning of a long life of public service. He served in both houses of Congress, as minister to Russia, minister to Great Britain, and as secretary of state.

Buchanan began his political career as a Federalist, but he believed in the Jacksonian principles and became a Democrat. Twice the name of Buchanan was proposed for President—in the campaigns of 1844 and 1852—before finally, in 1856, he was elected. Questions arising over slavery were increasing and becoming more troublesome to both North and South. The Dred Scott decision, denying the right of citizenship to a Negro, angered the North. Buchanan felt that slavery was right under the Constitution, but he believed that morally it was a great evil. Believing in the strict interpretation of the Constitution, he based his decisions upon the letter rather than the spirit of that great document. Critical questions imperiled the nation and Buchanan hesitated to make decisions which might precipitate trouble.

Before Buchanan left the presidency South Carolina seceded from the Union, the Confederate States were organized, and war threatened between the North and the South.

Defeated for re-election, Buchanan turned his heavy responsibilities over to one who had yet to prove his great fitness for the task—Abraham Lincoln. He spent the remaining seven years of his life at his home, "Wheatland," Pennsylvania.

Photo from "Acme"

ABRAHAM LINCOLN

16th President

Born February 12, 1809   Died April 15, 1865

President 1861-April 15, 1865

From the rude log cabin near Hodgenville, Kentucky, where Abraham Lincoln was born, the Lincoln family moved first to Indiana and then to Illinois. The wilderness of Kentucky and Indiana provided only snatches of schooling for Lincoln, but he read and reread the Bible and the few other books which he could get hold of.

Lincoln's boyhood wish to make the long trip down the Mississippi was realized after he moved to Indiana. In New Orleans he saw the slave market. At New Salem, Illinois, he clerked in a store, studied law, and took part in the political talk of the day. He also served in the Black Hawk War. After he began his practice of law he was elected to the Illinois legislature, and then to Congress.

Lincoln understood human nature, and he had a droll sense of humor which gave point to his arguments. In a series of famous debates with Stephen A. Douglas he upheld the principles of the Republican party. He cherished the Union, and he recognized that it was threatened by the great moral issues involved in the slavery question. After an address at Cooper Union, New York City, Lincoln rose to national prominence, and in 1860 was elected President.

In April, after his inauguration, the War between the States began. Lincoln met every crisis with poise and courage. In January, 1863, he issued the Emancipation Proclamation, freeing the slaves. Neither criticism nor praise turned him from the course he had chosen. He was re-elected in 1864. Early in 1865, Lincoln had the satisfaction of knowing that the Union had been preserved.

On the evening of April 14, while President and Mrs. Lincoln sat in their box at the Ford Theater, Lincoln was shot by John Wilkes Booth. After his death the following morning his secretary of war, Edwin M. Stanton, paid Lincoln a lasting tribute in the words, "Now he belongs to the ages."

Photo from Herbert Georg Studio, Springfield, Ill.

ANDREW JOHNSON

17th President

Born December 29, 1808   Died July 31, 1875

President April 15, 1865-1869

Raleigh, North Carolina, was the birthplace of Andrew Johnson. His parents were poor and he received little education.

Left fatherless when he was young, Johnson became a tailor's apprentice. A gentleman who often visited the tailor shop liked to read aloud the speeches of British statesmen and orators. These speeches interested the lad so much that, with the help of the visitor, he learned to read and spell. When a little older, Johnson moved to Tennessee, where he had his own tailor shop. There his young wife helped him to learn arithmetic and to write. Johnson was alert, successful in business, and interested in the affairs of his townsmen. He was elected alderman, then mayor of the town of Greeneville. Finally, as a friend of laboring men, he was elected to the Tennessee legislature, then to Congress, and later he was made governor of Tennessee.

Johnson's manner was frequently very brusque, although his convictions were honest and sincere. A southern Democrat, his views were never restricted by regional or partisan sympathies. He placed his faith in the Union. When every one of his southern colleagues withdrew early in 1861 from the Senate, Johnson alone held his post. This act enraged the South, but it gave him political strength in the North. President Lincoln rewarded his loyalty to the Union by making him military governor of Tennessee. Two years later he was elected vice president with Lincoln.

Lincoln's sudden death thrust Johnson into presidential responsibilities that would have challenged the wisdom of Lincoln himself. For Johnson they meant political disaster. Congress impeached him but did not succeed in removing him from office. He was not, however, re-elected.

Returning a few years later to the United States Senate, Johnson lived but a short time.

ULYSSES SIMPSON GRANT

18th President

Born April 27, 1822   Died July 23, 1885

President 1869-1877

Ulysses Grant was born at Point Pleasant, Ohio.

Young Grant received a good education, and secured appointment to the Military Academy at West Point. When he was graduated he was the best rider in his class. His commission entitled him to a place in the cavalry, but as there were no vacancies, Grant enlisted in the infantry and was sent at once to the Southwest. He took active part in nearly every important battle of the War with Mexico. His military life gave him little chance to be with his family and Grant finally resigned from the army. Unfortunate in business, he became a clerk in his brothers' store at Galena, Illinois.

At the beginning of the War between the States, Grant volunteered on condition that he be given command of a regiment. To his courage and wise military tactics the Union was indebted for Lee's surrender of the Confederate Army on April 9, 1865. Grant's terms of surrender and his courteous treatment of General Lee and his troops won much admiration in both North and South.

The Republican party made Grant its candidate in the campaign of 1868, and he was elected President, although he was not eager for the honor. Reconstruction in the South still presented many difficult problems over which sharp disputes arose. The country faced grave financial troubles, and Grant and his cabinet were in disagreement over the foreign policies of the United States. However, Grant was re-elected for a second term.

Grant's courage was never greater than when, in failing health, he set about the task of writing the story of his life. He lost his fortune after he retired from the presidency, and he hoped that his writing would provide an income for his family. Through days of great suffering he completed his *Memoirs* only a short time before his death, which occurred at his home, Mount McGregor, New York.

RUTHERFORD BIRCHARD HAYES

19th President

Born October 4, 1822   Died January 17, 1893

President 1877-1881

In the town of Delaware, Ohio, Rutherford Birchard Hayes was born, after his father died. An uncle gave him loving guidance, and the financial help which enabled him to get a good education.

Very early this young Ohioan, of New England and Scottish descent, showed an interest in books and a determination to improve his mind. He was conservative in thought and action. He never imposed his views upon other people, but he was firm in defending them.

Slavery seemed wrong to this thoughtful young man. When the Whig party gradually merged into the Republican party, Hayes found congenial association with the new group. He supported Lincoln, answered his call for volunteers, and served valiantly as a commander in the War between the States. While he was yet in command, Ohio elected him to Congress. He served three terms, in all, as governor of his state, standing firmly back of every measure that seemed to him definitely progressive and sound. He won the faith and esteem of political leaders and of people generally.

Republican leaders knew that Hayes had political strength and they nominated him for President. When the electoral votes were cast, the poll was so close that both sides claimed the victory, but Hayes finally won the election by just one vote. In his political appointments Hayes tried to be fair and honest. As a monetary policy he believed in maintaining a definite standard of value for every coined dollar. He did not compromise his views for political advantage, and he was opposed on principle to a President's serving a second term.

After leaving the President's office Hayes devoted his energy to educational enterprises and social betterment. He died at his home in Fremont, Ohio.

JAMES ABRAM GARFIELD

20th President

Born November 19, 1831   Died September 19, 1881

President 1881—September 19, 1881

Garfield's early life is a remarkable record of self-earned successes. He was born in a log cabin in Cuyahoga County, Ohio, of sturdy American pioneer parents. His father died when Garfield was two years old. The young lad learned to struggle through his own problems. He worked hard and enthusiastically. Books were his good friends, and he combined work with study until he completed his schooling at Williams College, Massachusetts. At twenty-six Garfield returned to teach at the Institute at Hiram, Ohio, where he had gone to school, and soon became president of the school. He studied law while he taught, and was admitted to practice in 1859.

Garfield volunteered for service in the War between the States, and was given command of a regiment in which many of his students enlisted. He served so successfully that he was made a major general. The Republican party nominated him for Congress while he was still in military service, and for eight successive terms he was elected as representative from his Ohio district. He was a well-informed statesman, a gifted orator, and a political leader.

In 1880 Garfield was elected to the Senate, but before he took his seat he received the Republican nomination for President. His name was proposed as a compromise, with Chester A. Arthur for vice president. Both were elected, Garfield representing the "half-breeds" and Arthur, the "stalwarts," the two factions of the Republican party at that time.

But the compromise which made Garfield President also foreshadowed his doom. On July 2, 1881, one of the many disappointed men who had hoped for political jobs at the hands of the opposing group, shot President Garfield. Garfield made a brave fight for life, lingering until September 19.

CHESTER ALAN ARTHUR

21st President

Born October 5, 1830   Died November 18, 1886

President September 19, 1881-1885

Chester Alan Arthur was born at Fairfield, Vermont. His Scotch-Irish father was a scholarly clergyman. At eighteen young Arthur was through college. For a time he taught school and studied law. During the War between the States he served in administrative positions. He became thoroughly familiar with politics and political "machine" organization.

Arthur was able, energetic, and in favor with the Republican party. Under Grant and Hayes he held the important post of collector of customs at the port of New York. Hundreds of small jobs came under his control. When President Hayes tried to bring this post under civil service, Arthur fought to continue the political "spoils system," and Hayes removed him from office. Arthur was an efficient administrator, but he became more and more a "machine" politician.

The election of Arthur as vice president, with President Garfield, was a compromise to satisfy both the "half-breeds" and the "stalwarts," the two Republican groups. Upon Garfield's death Arthur, who represented the "stalwarts," became President.

The country was in the midst of industrial and commercial expansion. During Arthur's administration three transcontinental railroads were completed, new plans were under discussion for the building of the Panama Canal, and the whole country was in a state of unparalleled growth and prosperity. The legislative branch of the government could scarcely keep pace with the complicated problems brought about by the rapid development of trusts, industrial expansion, transportation, and commerce. Arthur conducted the affairs of government with credit to himself and to the administration, but he lost the support of his own political group and was not re-elected.

At the end of his term Arthur retired to his home in New York City where he died two years later.

          Photo from "Acme"

GROVER CLEVELAND
22d & 24th President

Born March 18, 1837   Died June 24, 1908

President 1885-1889, 1893-1897

Grover Cleveland's father, a clergyman, died when his son was sixteen years old. By then the family had moved from Cleveland's birthplace at Caldwell, New Jersey, to central New York State. Since Cleveland had to help support his mother, he did not enlist in the War between the States. An uncle helped him secure work in Buffalo, where he studied law and was admitted to practice.

Politically Cleveland was a Democrat. He was successively assistant district attorney, county sheriff, and mayor of Buffalo. In each office he gained popular good will by fearlessly carrying on needed reforms. Because of this, he won many Republican votes in his campaign for the governorship of New York. Before he completed his term as governor his party nominated him for President and he was elected.

At this time a surplus in the national treasury gave political opponents a chance to criticise the tariff policy then in effect. The surplus encouraged political patronage and was the basis for hundreds of legislative bills. Cleveland vetoed one pension bill after another. Labor troubles and strikes began to attract nation-wide attention. Meanwhile Cleveland was busy giving thought to monetary standards and to questions of immigration.

It was chiefly on the question of tariff, however, that Cleveland was defeated at the next presidential election, only to be re-elected on that same issue, after the Republicans had been in control for four years.

During his second term, Cleveland persuaded Great Britain to arbitrate the matter of boundaries in Venezuela under the Monroe Doctrine, he settled controversies over Canadian fisheries, and he kept peace with Spain over Cuban independence.

Cleveland retired after his second term to enjoy for more than a decade his home at Princeton, New Jersey.

BENJAMIN HARRISON

23rd President

Born August 20, 1833   Died March 13, 1901

President 1889-1893

Benjamin Harrison was born at North Bend, Ohio, near the home of his grandfather, William Henry Harrison. After he completed his schooling at Miami University, he studied law and moved to Indianapolis where he became one of the foremost lawyers in Indiana.

At the beginning of the War between the States Harrison helped to recruit men, and was given command of a regiment. Later he joined General Sherman's forces in Georgia. Before leaving the army he was made a brigadier general.

Returning to Indianapolis, Harrison resumed his law practice and was active in Republican state and national politics. He was more friendly to pension bills than President Cleveland and he favored a high protective tariff. The Republican leaders considered him a sound, conservative statesman. They needed a presidential candidate who could carry the vote in the doubtful middle western states, so they nominated and elected Harrison.

Harrison saw the need for civil-service reform, but political job seekers made the task difficult. His compromises pleased neither politicians nor extreme reformists. Farmers were displeased because they thought the administration favored manufacturers; money standards were unstable; and increased pension allowances were rapidly eating up the surplus in the national treasury. Important legislation of his term included the McKinley high-tariff bill, the silver purchase law, and the Sherman anti-trust law. Harrison successfully settled vexing questions with Great Britain, Germany, and Italy.

But the country was in a state of unrest. Cleveland was still popular and he defeated President Harrison who was a candidate for re-election. Again Harrison turned to his law practice. President McKinley sent him in 1899 as a delegate to the Hague Peace Conference. Two years later he died at his home in Indianapolis.

WILLIAM McKINLEY

25th President

Born January 29, 1843   Died September 14, 1901

President 1897—September 14, 1901

William McKinley was born at Niles, Ohio. He received a good education, although illness interrupted his college course. Recovering his health he later enlisted in the War between the States. At twenty-two he returned from the service with the rank of major. He completed his study of law, married, and began the practice of his profession at Canton, Ohio.

McKinley was a strong Republican. He had a kindly, unquestioning trust in his fellow-men, and dealt with people in a spirit of good will. While he was in Congress he was the author of a bill for high tariff which the following Democratic Congress replaced with one which lowered the tariff. But the panic of 1893 again made people look to the party not then in power to bring more prosperous times. McKinley was nominated and elected President against William Jennings Bryan, the "free silver" candidate of the Democratic party.

Gold was discovered in Alaska, and the Dingley tariff bill again raised the duties on foreign manufactures. Such great progress had been made in transportation, commerce, and industry that the machinery of government had not become adjusted to it. The country seemed in a prosperous state when the astonishing news came of the sinking of the U. S. battleship "Maine" at Havana, and war with Spain was declared. The United States soon won the war; gained the Philippines and independence for Cuba. But the Filipinos, far across the Pacific were not thought capable of self-government, and many problems arose before satisfactory plans were made to maintain their peace and security.

The gold standard was adopted in 1900. In November of that year the Republican Party elected McKinley for a second term. A few months later, as he was welcoming guests at the Pan-American Exposition in Buffalo, he was shot by an assassin. He lived only nine days.

THEODORE ROOSEVELT

26th President

Born October 27, 1858   Died January 6, 1919

President September 14, 1901–1909

The Roosevelt family, originally from Holland, had lived in New York City for many generations before Theodore Roosevelt was born there.

Roosevelt was a frail boy, but by constant physical training he developed into a rugged man. He became interested in government and politics. His broad interests and forceful personality commanded the attention of Republican leaders in New York, and he was elected to the state legislature.

After Roosevelt lost both his mother and his young wife, he spent some time on a North Dakota ranch where he explored the country and wrote. Shortly after his return to the East, President Harrison appointed him to serve on the civil service commission from which he resigned to become police commissioner of New York City. Later he was appointed assistant secretary of the navy. During the Spanish American War he won distinction with his famous Rough Riders. Elected governor of New York he vigorously opposed unfair business practices. Later he was elected to the office of vice president, but McKinley's assassination made him President.

As President, Roosevelt successfully arbitrated such disputes as the Alaskan boundaries and the anthracite coal strike, and he was awarded the Nobel Prize for his aid in the settlement of the war between Russia and Japan. He supported every measure for the conservation of natural resources and the building of the Panama Canal.

After a second term Roosevelt went exploring in the jungles of Africa and South America. On his return he led the Progressive party in the campaign of 1912, but later actively supported the Republican party.

Theodore Roosevelt exemplified a strenuous type of leadership and made valuable contributions in a variety of fields.

Photo, copyright by Clinedinst, Washington, D. C.

WILLIAM HOWARD TAFT

27th President

Born September 15, 1857   Died March 8, 1930

President 1909–1913

William Howard Taft was born in Cincinnati, Ohio. He was graduated from Yale with high honors, then studied law and began his practice at Cincinnati.

Before his marriage Taft had held several public offices, and afterward he became judge of the Ohio superior court. President Harrison, recognizing Taft's ability, appointed him a judge of the federal circuit court in Ohio, where he established an excellent reputation as a jurist. After the Spanish American War President McKinley appointed him first governor of the Philippines. He discharged his duties with great success and so devotedly that twice he refused an offer from President Theodore Roosevelt for appointment to the Supreme Court—a position he greatly coveted. Later he became secretary of war in the Roosevelt cabinet.

His own successes combined with the whole-hearted support of Theodore Roosevelt won the presidential election for Taft in 1908. Taft was not so strenuously progressive as Roosevelt, and the more progressive voters bitterly opposed the conservative group of "stand-patters." Taft's middle course pleased neither faction. However, during his term the Postal Savings Bank was created and parcel post inaugurated, the oil and tobacco trusts were dissolved, tax on corporations was levied, and the Department of Labor and the Children's Bureau were made separate and distinct departments of the government. In arbitration of questions with foreign countries Taft proved to be an able executive. But, as he failed to fulfill the political hopes of the progressive element of the Republican party, Taft was defeated for a second term.

He became professor of law at Yale, and took a leading part in promoting world peace. President Harding appointed him chief justice of the Supreme Court where for nine years he enjoyed this high honor. Ill health forced him to resign only a month before his death.

Photo, copyright by Clinedinst, Washington, D. C.

WOODROW WILSON

28th President

Born December 28, 1856   Died February 3, 1924

President 1913–1921

Woodrow Wilson, born at Staunton, Virginia, was of Scotch-Irish descent. After completing a law course and receiving the degree of doctor of philosophy from Johns Hopkins University, he spent many years as a professor in various universities of the East, finally becoming president of Princeton University. Wilson's special interest was in government and history, which furnished the themes for most of his writing. After his resignation as president of Princeton University he was elected governor of New Jersey. He became the choice of the Democratic party as the presidential candidate in 1912, and was elected President.

During Wilson's first term important legislation was passed which affected banking, trusts, tariff, farm credits and loans, labor, and income taxation.

Revolution in Mexico strained the friendly relations of the United States and that country for a time, but was finally settled. Meantime, war in Europe threatened the peace of the world. While many were urging American intervention in the European conflict, Wilson was exerting every possible influence for peace. "He kept us out of war," was the campaign slogan in 1916, and Wilson was re-elected for a second term. But after Germany declared unrestricted submarine warfare the United States entered the war. After the armistice was signed in November, 1918, Wilson went to Europe in person to present his famous "fourteen points" as a basis for a new world peace. He was the author of the League of Nations which the United States, alone of the great powers of the world, rejected. For his efforts toward permanent world peace he received the Nobel Prize in 1920.

In failing health, Wilson left the White House, but until his death, which occurred in Washington three years later, he continued to try to win the favor of his country for the League of Nations.

Photo from Clinedinst Studio, Washington, D. C.

WARREN GAMALIEL HARDING

29th President

Born November 2, 1865   Died August 2, 1923

President 1921–August 2, 1923

In a rural Ohio community Warren Gamaliel Harding was born, the son of a doctor of moderate means. He attended the near-by Ohio Central College at Iberia where he was editor of the school paper.

Harding learned the details of printing, editing, and publishing by actual practice, and before he was twenty he purchased the Daily Star at Marion, Ohio. He took a leading part in the business and political life of his community and state, and was unwavering in his loyalty to the Republican party. He served in the state Senate and later, in the United States Senate, he performed valuable service on a number of important committees.

Harding became a prominent candidate for the presidency and was elected to succeed Woodrow Wilson. He faced reconstruction along many lines, following the World War. He disapproved of American representation in the League of Nations, but he wanted America to take part in the deliberations at the Hague for a permanent World Court. The Limitation of Armaments conference at Washington, to which Harding invited representatives from all interested countries, was an outstanding accomplishment of his administration.

With perfect confidence in the men he had chosen for his cabinet, President Harding entrusted to them grave responsibilities that involved the capital wealth of the country. In betrayal of this trust a few high officials drew the President and the administration into the unpleasant "Teapot Dome" and several other scandals. President Harding did not live to face the full blast of the revelations. Soon after suspicion was cast upon the dealings of these men, the President made a trip to Alaska and on his return was fatally stricken in San Francisco.

         Photo, copyright by Harris & Ewing

CALVIN COOLIDGE

30th President

Born July 4, 1872   Died January 5, 1933

President August 2, 1923–1929

Calvin Coolidge was born on a farm in Plymouth, Vermont. His parents were thrifty New Englanders. Coolidge learned the routine of farm life along with his schooling and finally entered Amherst College where he was graduated with honors.

When Coolidge left college he entered a law office at Northampton, Massachusetts. There he read law for two years and was admitted to practice. Through a number of minor public offices he proved himself worthy of public responsibilities. He served in both houses of the Massachusetts legislature and was governor of Massachusetts for two terms. His settlement of the Boston police strike attracted the attention of the nation.

The simplicity and the homely virtues of Calvin Coolidge impressed Americans. The Republican party decided that he would be helpful to the ticket as the vice-presidential candidate, with Warren G. Harding. As vice president, he presided over the United States Senate in a manner acceptable to the Democrats as well as to the members of his own party.

A few hours after word was received of President Harding's death, Coolidge received the oath of office as President from his father, a justice of the peace at Plymouth, Vermont. Coolidge's first task was the clearing up of the "Teapot Dome" scandal. His rigid governmental economies made it possible to reduce the public debt and scale down the federal income tax. The Kellogg-Briand Peace Pact, outlawing war as an instrument for settling international disputes, was an achievement of Coolidge's second term.

Coolidge's firm declaration, "I do not choose to run for President in 1928," made the Republican party and the country understand that he wished to retire from public life. From his home in Northampton, Massachusetts, he wrote and was active in business until his death.

       Photo, copyright by Harris & Ewing

HERBERT CLARK HOOVER

31st President

Born August 10, 1874   Died October 20, 1964

President 1929–1933

Herbert Hoover, son of a village blacksmith of West Branch, Iowa, was left an orphan when he was nine. He grew up in the home of his Quaker uncle in Oregon and later studied mining engineering at Leland Stanford University.

After several years of practical experience in the mines of the Southwest, he went to Australia, then circled the globe, holding various positions as a mining expert and administrator.

During the first part of the World War Hoover successfully directed Belgian relief. After the United States entered the war, President Wilson appointed him national food administrator. He managed the distribution of surplus foods of the United States to the starving millions in stricken European countries after the war. This work brought him in contact with statesmen all over the world.

As yet, Hoover had not declared any political party allegiance. Democrats and Republicans alike looked to him for help in great emergencies. He served ably as food administrator under Wilson and as secretary of commerce under Harding and Coolidge. He had never been elected to a political office, but he seemed to be the logical man for the next President. The Republican party secured his candidacy and he was elected.

But Hoover could not prevent the economic, political, and social disturbance that followed. It was world-wide. In the United States the stock market crashed after a period of wild speculation. President Hoover set up boards and established commissions to deal with special domestic and foreign problems in an effort to revive business. He proposed a moratorium on war debts between nations.

As ever, people looked to the party not then in power to restore order and prosperity. Hoover, defeated for a second term, returned to his home at Palo Alto, California.

FRANKLIN DELANO ROOSEVELT

32nd President

Born January 30, 1882   Died April 12, 1945

President 1933–April 12, 1945

Franklin Roosevelt was the only child of an old and wealthy family. He enjoyed the advantages of an excellent and extensive education. Despite the severe physical handicap of infantile paralysis, Roosevelt, for thirty-five years, carried on a colorful political career.

First elected President of the United States in 1932, his twelve years in that capacity thrust upon him many of the most crucial controversial decisions of our times. Following the worst economic depression in our history, Roosevelt led his countrymen in the way he believed best, calling his plan and philosophy the "New Deal." Never, perhaps, has a single plan of action carried within its influence such great differences of opinion—deep devotion and intense bitterness.

Very soon after the President's re-election in 1936 an impending war in Europe seemed inevitable. Following the 1939 invasion of Poland, Roosevelt's chief concerns became foreign affairs. On December 7, 1941, came a tragic ending to months of anxious tension and attempted peace negotiations. With the surprise attack on Pearl Harbor, Hawaii, the United States Congress declared war on the Japanese Empire. Four days later Italy and Germany announced declarations of war on the United States.

The remaining years of Franklin Roosevelt's presidency and life were spent at conference tables all over the world. He traveled to meetings with leaders of all the allied nations. Although he was constantly required to take decisive action in the waging of a terrible war, plans were ever in the making for a world of peace when the conflict could be ended.

Before the conclusion of any of these struggles, on April 12, 1945, just eighty-three days after the opening of his fourth term, the President died suddenly at his Warm Springs, Georgia, home.

Photo, Copyright by Harris & Ewing

HARRY S. TRUMAN
33rd President

Born May 8, 1884   Died December 26, 1972

President 1945–1953

Harry Truman was born in Lamar, Missouri, and educated in the public schools of Independence. He was a student at the Kansas City School of Law. From 1926 to 1934 he served as presiding judge of Jackson County. In 1934 he was elected to the United States Senate and served for seven years. Although interested and active in promoting transportation and railroad legislation, perhaps he was best known as chairman of the Senate Committee to Investigate the National Defense Program.

Having served a brief term as vice president, on April 12, 1945, within four hours of Franklin Roosevelt's death, Harry Truman became President. The new executive was immediately confronted with the winning of a great war. Twenty-seven days after taking office, he declared the unconditional surrender of Germany. Following the use of man's first atomic bombs, President Truman, on August 10, 1945, announced Japanese acceptance of surrender terms.

With the conclusion of World War II, the new President was plunged into the difficult problems of reconversion at home as well as peace settlements abroad. Serious industrial strikes threatened to paralyze the American economy. Demobilization of the greatest army and navy in history, and no further demand for war materials, caused apprehension over unemployment. The bitter struggle over price controls split many groups. Meanwhile the world situation remained chaotic and uncertain. Quarrels occurred between the United States and the Soviet Union over United Nations policies.

In 1948, Harry Truman was elected President. He was soon faced with another impending war. On June 25, 1950, the President ordered American troops to enter Korea as part of the United Nations forces.

After seven years, President Truman announced to the American public that he considered he had finished his service to his country and would not be available as the Democratic nominee for President in 1952.

DWIGHT DAVID EISENHOWER
34th President

Born October 14, 1890   Died March 28, 1969

President 1953–1961

Dwight David Eisenhower, born in Denison, Texas, was reared and educated in Abilene, Kansas, amidst the influences of a rugged frontier town and a deeply religious home. Eisenhower was appointed in 1911 to the United States Military Academy at West Point. He was graduated in 1915 and began an army career marked by a series of assignments in a wide range of military experiences which soon won him recognition.

In November, 1942, having risen to the rank of Lieutenant General, Eisenhower commanded the American forces landing in North Africa and soon after became Supreme Commander of Allied Expeditionary Forces. In this capacity he directed the attack on the Normandy coast in 1944 by land, sea, and air—the greatest mass invasion in history.

In May, 1945, after signing the unconditional surrender concluding the war in Europe, Eisenhower became military governor of the U.S. Occupied Zone in Germany. A few months later he returned to the United States to succeed Gen. Marshall as U.S. Army Chief of Staff.

Retiring from active service, Eisenhower became President of Columbia University in 1948. When the North Atlantic Treaty Organization (NATO) was formed, he was recalled in 1950 to act as supreme allied commander in Europe. In 1952 he was "drafted" by the Republican party to become their candidate for the Presidency. On Nov. 4, 1952, he won the election by a very large majority.

The outstanding achievements of President Eisenhower's first administration were: the armistice in the Korean War, the strengthening of NATO, and the Geneva Conference of 1955. In 1956 he was reelected to the Presidency, again defeating Adlai E. Stevenson.

Highlights of his second term were: the launching of space satellites, the declaration of the Eisenhower doctrine for the preservation of peace in the Middle East (1957), the opening of the St. Lawrence Seaway (1959) and his good-will tour to allied European, Asian and African nations (1959).

JOHN FITZGERALD KENNEDY

35th President

Born May 29, 1917   Died November 22, 1963

President 1961–1963

John F. Kennedy, born in Brookline, Massachusetts, was the first Roman Catholic ever to be elected to the Presidency. A strong factor in his winning this high office was his use of television during his campaign, when he debated political issues with Richard Nixon.

John Kennedy was educated in the public schools of Brookline, the Choate School, the London School of Economics, and Harvard and Stanford universities.

In World War II, Kennedy served in the Navy as a PT boat commander in the South Pacific. He was seriously injured in service, and was decorated with the Navy and Marine Corps medal, as well as the Purple Heart.

His political career began in 1946 with his election to the U.S. House of Représentatives as a Congressman. He was twice re-elected to the House. In 1952 he ran for the Senate and won. In 1958 he was re-elected by a record margin of votes.

In 1960 Kennedy became the youngest man (age 43) ever elected President. He called his program "The New Frontier," and vigorously tried to implement his plans. Not all were successful, but he was instrumental in launching the U.S. Peace Corps. During his administration the 23rd Amendment to the Constitution was ratified. It gave the residents of the District of Columbia the right to vote in national elections. Also, the hourly wage rate was raised to $1.25.

While in office he was faced by the Berlin crisis and the Cuban crisis; both incidents brought with them the threat of war.

He was respected and admired in many lands around the world, as well as in his own country. Then, on a sunny day in Dallas, Texas, on November 22, 1963, he was shot to death by an assassin's bullets. The whole free world mourned the passing of so gifted and dedicated a leader.

LYNDON BAINES JOHNSON
36th President

Born August 27, 1908   Died January 22, 1973
President 1963–1969

Lyndon B. Johnson was born in a farm near Stonewall, Texas. He attended public schools in Johnson City, and graduated from Southwest Texas State Teachers College.

After two years' teaching school he began his political career as secretary to a Texas Congressman. In 1935 F. D. Roosevelt named him Texas Director of the National Youth Administration, and in 1937 he was elected to a vacancy in the U.S. House of Representatives. Johnson was the first Congressman to go into uniform after Pearl Harbor as a Navy officer in the South Pacific and was decorated for gallantry.

In 1948 he was elected to the U.S. Senate and served there until 1960, the last 8 years as Democratic leader.

John F. Kennedy picked Johnson as his Vice President in 1960 and upon Kennedy's assassination November 22, 1963, Johnson assumed the Presidency. His greatest strength as President was his skill in legislative relations and he won Congressional approval of a civil rights act, a major education bill, and the economic opportunity act which launched his "War on Poverty."

Elected President in his own right in 1964 by the largest majority in history, Johnson pushed through "The Great Society" program, including medical care for the aged and civil rights acts guaranteeing open housing.

But Johnson's terms were marred by racial riots and street protests resulting from the increasing U.S. involvement in the Viet Nam War.

Considered a "Hawk" by those "Doves" desiring immediate peace in Viet Nam, Johnson on March 31, 1968 refused to run for re-election, and announced a partial curtailment of bombing of North Viet Nam.

Johnson's six years in office probably saw more social reforms enacted than in any comparable period of U.S. history.

RICHARD MILHOUS NIXON
37th President

Born January 9, 1913   Died April 22, 1994

President 1969–1974

Richard M. Nixon was born at Yorba Linda, California, of Quaker parentage. He attended public school in Whittier, California, and graduated with honors from Whittier College and the Duke University Law School.

He practiced law in Whittier until Pearl Harbor, then volunteered in the Navy, winning two South Pacific Battle stars and two commendations.

In 1946 Nixon was elected to Congress, where he gained national prominence by pressing for a House investigation of Alger Hiss. Elected to the Senate in 1950, he became Dwight D. Eisenhower's Republican running mate in 1952. As Vice President he visited 56 countries, including the Soviet Union where he had his famous "kitchen debate" with Nikita Khrushchev.

In 1960 Nixon ran for President but lost to John F. Kennedy. Two years later he ran unsuccessfully for governor of California and "retired" from politics, moving to New York City to practice law. But he was again nominated for President in 1968 and was elected.

Inflation, rising unemployment, the Viet Nam conflict, and the Watergate scandal were the major problems during the Nixon Administration.

Active fighting in Viet Nam ceased during Nixon's Presidency, and he was the first Chief Executive to visit the People's Republic of China. An independent postal system was also established, laws to save the environment were enacted, and he supported laws for revenue sharing and welfare reform. His new Chief Justice, Warren Burger, ushered in a conservative court era. Strategic Arms Limitation talks, the Nuclear Non-Proliferation Treaty, and the first Apollo lunar landing were other high points of his term in office.

As a result of the Watergate scandal, Nixon resigned his Presidency on August 8, 1974. He was the first Chief Executive of the United States to do so.

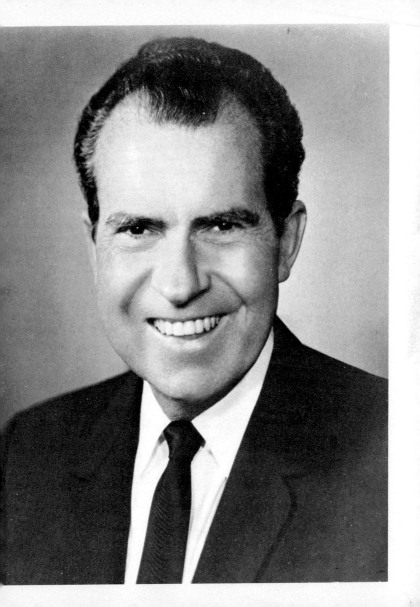

GERALD RUDOLPH FORD
38th President

Born July 14, 1913

President 1974–1977

Born in Omaha, Nebraska, and raised in Grand Rapids, Michigan, President Ford was an honor graduate of the University of Michigan in 1935, starred on its football team, and went on to the Yale University Law School, from which he was graduated in 1941. During World War II, he served as a lieutenant commander in the U.S. Navy aboard the Aircraft Carrier *Monterey*. Later he returned to Grand Rapids to practice law.

In 1948 he was elected as a Republican to the House of Representatives from the Fifth Michigan Congressional District and was re-elected for 12 more terms. From 1964 until December 6, 1973, when he was sworn in as Vice President to replace Spiro Agnew, he served as Minority Leader of the House.

Obstruction of justice charges in the Watergate burglary of Democratic campaign offices brought on a serious national crisis, and on August 8, 1974, Nixon became the first man to resign the Presidency. The next day Ford was sworn in as President.

During his administration, Ford was faced with such tasks as restoring confidence in the Presidency, inflation, a crippled economy, an energy crisis, and the threat of conflict in the Middle East.

Known for his outstanding political and legislative acumen, President Ford quickly impressed the nation with his openness, candor, and sincerity, which he maintained throughout his term of office.

Even though it jeopardized his popularity, Ford granted a full pardon to Richard Nixon in an effort to close the books on the Watergate scandal. He also announced a program of leniency for draft evaders and deserters in an attempt to end the bitterness of the Viet Nam conflict.

JIMMY CARTER

39th President

Born October 1, 1924

President 1977-1981

Jimmy Carter was born October 1, 1924, in Plains, Georgia, a small town in the southwestern part of the state. His father, James Earl Carter, Sr., was a farmer; his mother, Lillian, is a nurse.

President Carter was educated in the Plains public schools, entered the Naval ROTC program at Georgia Institute of Technology, and was graduated from the U.S. Naval Academy in 1947. In 1952 he did postgraduate work at Union College in Schenectady, New York.

During his naval career he was stationed in California, Virginia, Hawaii, and Connecticut. Later he was assigned to the nuclear submarine program directed by Admiral Hyman Rickover.

Following his father's death in 1953, Carter resigned his commission and returned to Plains to run the family peanut farm and warehouse. He also started a fertilizer and seed business which grew into a profitable enterprise.

In 1962 he was elected to the Georgia Senate, and in 1970 he was elected Georgia's 76th governor. While in this office he visited a number of countries in Latin America, Western Europe, and the Middle East. As a member of the Trilateral Commission, he periodically met with leaders from Western Europe, North America, and Japan to discuss matters of mutual interest. His fellow governors selected him to serve as chairman of the Southern Regional Education Board, the Appalachian Regional Commission, the Coastal Plains Regional Action Planning Commission, and the Southern Growth Policies Board.

In 1973 he became the Democratic Party's National Chairman for the 1974 elections. On December 12, 1974, he announced his candidacy for President and won his party's nomination at the 1976 Democratic National Convention. On November 2, 1976, he was elected President with 297 electoral votes and 50.1 percent of the popular votes.

RONALD WILSON REAGAN

40th President

Born February 6, 1911

President 1981-1989

Ronald Wilson Reagan was born February 6, 1911, in Tampico, Illinois, the son of Nellie Wilson Reagan and John Reagan. He was educated in Illinois public schools and was graduated from Eureka College (Ill.) in 1931, with a degree in economics and sociology.

Following a brief career as a sports broadcaster and editor, Reagan moved to California to work in motion pictures. His film career, interrupted by three years of service in the Army Air Corps during World War II, encompassed 50 feature-length motion pictures. He served six terms as president of the Screen Actors Guild and two terms as president of the Motion Picture Industry Council.

In 1966 Ronald Reagan began his public service career with his election as Governor of California. In 1969, he was chairman of the Republican Governors Association and in 1970, he was elected to a second term as Governor.

In 1975 he announced his candidacy for the 1976 presidential nomination. After the election, which he lost narrowly, he renewed his nationally syndicated radio commentary program, newspaper column, and national speaking schedule which he had started after serving as Governor.

In November 1979 Ronald Reagan announced his candidacy for the 1980 presidential nomination; he was nominated unanimously on the first ballot at the Republican National Convention in July 1980. He was elected and on January 20, 1981, was sworn in as the 40th President of the United States. In 1984 he was re-elected to a second term as President.

Reagan has received a number of awards, including the National Humanitarian Award from the National Conference of Christians and Jews, City of Hope "Torch of Life" Award for Humanitarian Service, Horatio Alger Award, American Newspaper Guild Award, Freedoms Foundations Awards, Distinguished American Award from the National Football Foundation Hall of Fame, American Patriots Hall of Fame, and Medal of Valor of the State of Israel.

GEORGE HERBERT WALKER BUSH

41st President

Born June 12, 1924

President 1989–1993

George Herbert Walker Bush was born in Milton, Massachusetts, and graduated from Phillips Academy in Andover, Massachusetts. He enlisted in the U.S. Navy Reserve on his 18th birthday, during the Second World War, and received his wings and commission while still 18 years old. During his term of service in the Pacific Theater (August 1942–September 1945), he received the Distinguished Flying Cross and three Air Medals.

After graduation from Yale University in 1948, Mr. Bush moved to Texas, where he pursued a career in the petroleum industry.

Mr. Bush was elected to the U.S. House of Representatives in 1966 from Texas' 7th District. He was re-elected to the House two years later.

Mr. Bush's reputation as a leader in international affairs grew during the 1970's. In 1971, he was named U.S. Ambassador to the United Nations, a position he held until 1973, when he became Chairman of the Republican National Committee. In October 1974, Mr. Bush traveled to Beijing, where he served as Chief of the U.S. Liaison Office during the critical period when the United States renewed ties with the People's Republic of China. In 1976, he was appointed Director of Central Intelligence, and was given credit for strengthening the intelligence community and helping to restore morale at the CIA.

From 1981 to 1988, Bush served as Vice President under Ronald Reagan. During his term he coordinated the administration's activities to combat international terrorism, and headed similar efforts on the Presidential Task Force on Regulatory Relief and the National Narcotics Border Interdiction System (NNBIS).

In the 1988 election, with Indiana Senator J. Danforth (Dan) Quayle as his running mate, Bush won a landslide Electoral College victory (426–112).

WILLIAM JEFFERSON CLINTON
42nd President

Born August 19, 1946

President 1993– *2000*

Bill Clinton was born in Hope, Arkansas three months after the death of his father, William Jefferson Blythe, III. At the age of 15, Clinton legally adopted his stepfather's surname. He graduated from Georgetown University, attended Oxford University, in England, as a Rhodes Scholar, and received his law degree from Yale University in 1972.

From 1973 to 1976, Clinton taught law at the University of Arkansas at Fayetteville. He was involved in the presidential campaigns of George S. McGovern, in 1972, and Jimmy Carter, in 1976.

Mr. Clinton had a distinguished career in state politics: He served as attorney general of Arkansas from 1976–78. In 1978, at the age of 32, he became the youngest governor of Arkansas, at the time a two-year position. Although defeated in 1980, he was reelected in 1982, and served as governor from 1983 until 1992, when he was elected to the Presidency in the middle of his fourth term. As governor, he worked to improve educational opportunities, health care for children, and for requiring job-training for welfare recipients.

Nationally, as chairman of the National Governors' Association, and later as head of the Democratic Leadership Council, Clinton worked to influence the Democratic Party's move toward a more conservative, centrist political position.

Clinton received the Democratic Presidential nomination in 1992, from a field of five candidates. He selected Senator Al Gore (D, Tennessee) as his running mate.

The 1992 campaign against incumbent George Bush was notable for the entry of a strong third-party candidate, H. Ross Perot, who drew support from the disaffected right as well as from the economically conservative "Reagan Democrats" who formed a portion of the Republican candidate's support. Emphasizing such domestic issues, as access to health care, economic growth, the environment, and renewal of the nation's infrastructure Mr. Clinton managed to pull together a somewhat splintered Democratic Party, winning about 48% of the popular vote and achieving an electoral victory.

THE INDEX